SUFFRAGETTES

SUFFRAGETTES

How Britain's women fought
& died for the right to vote

FRANK MEERES

AMBERLEY

This edition first published 2014

Amberley Publishing
The Hill, Stroud
Gloucestershire, GL5 4EP

www.amberley-books.com

Copyright © Frank Meeres, 2013, 2014

The right of Frank Meeres to be identified as the Author
of this work has been asserted in accordance with the
Copyrights, Designs and Patents Act 1988.

British Library Cataloguing in Publication Data.
A catalogue record for this book is available from the British Library.

ISBN 978 1 4456 3390 9 (paperback)
ISBN 978 1 4456 2057 2 (ebook)

Typesetting and Origination by Amberley Publishing
Printed in Great Britain

Contents

Introduction

The First World War was the first war that could be called total: it involved all men but also a large number of women, many of whom had to fight against male indifference or antagonism for their right to play a part.

Many women naturally took up the traditional role of females in wartime – attending the wounded, either in England or abroad. War hospitals were set up and many stately homes were given up by their owners for use as hospitals. Many thousands of women served in them, whether as nurses or in less skilled but equally necessary roles such as cleaners and cooks. Some nurses served behind the lines on the Western Front or in the Near East. A number even lost their lives, either from stray shells hitting casualty clearing stations or when the ships in which they were travelling were torpedoed. Over 100,000 women were involved in nursing during the First World War.

The most famous nurse was Edith Cavell, who was already working in Brussels when war broke out. She remained there after the city was captured by the Germans, and nursed soldiers of all nationalities – and also helped Allied soldiers to escape through enemy lines, for which she was shot in October 1915. Her execution, whether or not it was justified on legal grounds, was a great mistake politically: her death aroused anger in many countries throughout the world, and was used as a recruitment tool by the British Army.

Conscription of men to serve in the forces created an opportunity that women were quick to exploit, moving into jobs that had previously been closed to them. Many made munitions – this was difficult and dangerous work, affecting the health of those employed: the chemicals turned the skin yellow so that the girls were nicknamed 'canaries'. There were many fatalities among munitions workers, whose sacrifice in the war effort has been largely forgotten: 105 people were killed in an explosion at Faversham in 1916, and 73 at Silvertown, West Ham, in 1917. The greatest number of fatalities in a single explosion occurred at Chilwell, Nottingham, in July 1918: 134 people were killed. Altogether, about 800,000 women worked in some engineering role, mainly in munitions, during the war.

There were many other jobs for women to fill. Many worked on the land – although the Women's Land Army is associated with the Second World War in most minds, it actually began in the First World War, and over 250,000 women worked on the land in the war. They took over a wide range of other jobs as well, such as bus conductors, postal workers, drivers of carts or of motor cars.

Women could even join the Armed Forces, signing up in an auxiliary branch of the Army, the Women's Auxiliary Army Corps, later called the Queen Mary's Auxiliary Army Corps. This was followed in 1918 by the Women's Royal Naval Service and the Women's Royal Air Force. Women in these units were not trained to use weapons, but served in many other capacities, thus freeing up men for front-line duties. About 100,000 women were in the auxiliary forces in the war.

Not all women supported the war when it broke out: their experiences in the suffragette movement, and in some cases their links with suffragette groups in other countries, emboldened some women to take an anti-war stance. Some of these women worked with the Independent Labour Party, also opposed to the war; others found their role in the National Federation of Women Workers, defending the interests of women in the workplace. 'Fed', as it was affectionately known, had been founded by Mary Macarthur and its other leaders included Margaret Bondfield, Susan Lawrence and Dorothy Jewson, all three of whom became MPs in 1923.

With women playing so many key roles during the war, it seemed absurd that they should not be allowed the vote. Lord Haldane, himself a former Minister of War, said in the House of Lords on 9 January 1918,

The magnitude of the war, the kind of organisation up against which we find ourselves, is of a nature which has made it necessary to mobilise the whole nation. To-day we are a nation in arms. Women, although they are not really fighting in the trenches, are in arms as men are in arms, as part of the great supply system of the Army without which the Army could not fight, or the Navy either. Women are taking a tremendous part in this war. They are sacrificing their health, their lungs, they are sacrificing everything, to throw themselves into the work, and they have thrown themselves into it with an integrity of purpose and with a determination to make the right prevail which certainly does not put them anywhere behind the other sex ... There have been women, like Edith Cavell, whose names will not be forgotten, women who died under shell fire, died under bombardment, died by bullet wounds, just as have men have died. They have shown courage and determination which ... puts them on a level with the other sex in this matter.

Britain in 1918 was a very different place to Britain in 1914, and one great difference was in the attitudes of men towards women and their place in society. However, the vote had not been easily won: this book tells the story of the struggle by women in the first fifteen years of the century to obtain this right.

*

In Britain today, it is taken for granted that every adult has the right to vote for their Member of Parliament and for their local council. Imagine what it would be like to have no say in who governed you; this is what it was like for women for most of this country's history. Their condition could be likened to slavery, and many women did make this parallel. Charlotte Carmichael Stopes observed in 1908 that 'patriots are never weary of singing "Britons never, never shall be slaves". Of course, they should not be so. But they forget that every Briton, who happens to be born a woman, is according to the definition doomed to be a slave. *Slavery consists in having to obey laws in the making of which one has no voice*. Therefore, all British women are slaves today. Their payments are not the taxes of a free people, but the tribute of a conquered and subject race. A sad, unconsidered result of this state of affairs is that no man born of a slave-woman can really free himself until his mother is emancipated.' Women had played a major role in campaigns to abolish the slave trade and later the institution itself, figures such as Hannah More, Elizabeth Fry and Elizabeth Heyrick leading the way. Now it was time for women to free themselves.

One of the suffragette leaders, Christabel Pankhurst, saw the right to vote as a symbol of the role of women as a whole: 'The vote is the symbol of freedom and equality. Any class which is denied the vote is branded as an inferior class. Women's disenfranchisement is to them a perpetual lesson in servility, and to men it teaches arrogance and injustice where their dealings with women are concerned.' A century ago, many women were convinced that this was wrong and they decided to fight for the right to vote, some even being prepared to go to prison for their beliefs.

What was it like to go to prison a century ago? This is the experience of Hannah Mitchell, sent to prison in Manchester in 1906:

The basement of the Manchester Police Court was then, and still is, a horrible place to wait in, like a cattle stall with bars in front. One other woman went with us in the van to Strangeways. She was being sent to prison for fighting with her neighbours. 'I only called her cow,' she told us, 'and so she is.' She gave us her opinion of the police in language which coincided with my own thoughts on the subject. We all felt that we had not even half-a-crown's worth of defiance out of the affair, as we had no intention of clashing with the police at Belle Vue, but we mentally vowed that next time the law should have something to complain of.

At Strangeways, we were not badly treated, being excused the bath which our fellow prisoner was compelled to take. We heard her loudly complaining that the water was cold and dirty and there was no soap. The wardress kindly allowed us to change in her own room, giving us a sheet to use as a screen. The prison dress was horrible, coarse and unshapely. It consisted of a wide skirt, thickly gathered at the waist, a sort of short jacket or bed gown, such as was worn a hundred years ago, in a horrible drab stuff stamped with a black arrow, one flannel singlet, a coarse calico chemise, no knickers, or corsets, short thick stockings without garters and heavy shoes which would have fitted a navvy; mine were different sizes. There was a blue check apron with a sort of check duster for a handkerchief. Even our hairpins were taken away, and we were compelled to push our hair into a prison cap. This cap was the only decent thing given to us. Adela [Pankhurst, a fellow prisoner] whispered to me that I looked like a queen in mine. I did not feel very queenly; ugly dress makes one feel uncomfortable. It was all too big, and the absence of garters and knickers made one feel almost naked.

We all had a sort of numbered badge; mine was H.10, the number of my cell. The cell itself was not too unpleasant, and quite clean. There were two blankets and a straw mattress which would have been comfortable enough but too short, being only long enough for a child's cot. However, I was so tired that I slept fairly well until the bell rang at 6 a.m., when the door was unlocked, and we were ordered out to the lavatories where we washed and emptied our slops. We were then taken out for exercise, so called, which meant just walking round and round in a circle, without being allowed to speak to each other. I found this very hard, as my shoes kept slipping off, and the stockings, also much too big, fell down over my ankles. When I returned to the cell, I remedied this by tearing up the rags given to me to polish my 'tins' with, and using them for garters. I think I was then expected to 'make my bed' by rolling up the bedding and stacking it along with the bed against the wall. Instead I just sat on the bed, not caring very much what happened next. I was feeling very ill, having had no food since lunch on the previous day. A tin mug of gruel and a small brown loaf were handed in. The gruel was not too bad, but the bread was quite uneatable. If it had been of sawdust, flavoured with road sweepings, it could not have not tasted worse. My head ached terribly, and I would have given anything for a cup of tea.

But when the door was opened by the Deputy Governor, a woman, and I was told to get ready to go out, as my fine had been paid, I was very angry, and refused to go. She urged me to go, saying kindly that prison was no place for women like me. I found my one decent suit rolled up in a bundle as if it were the rags of some drunken tramp.

I was not pleased to find my husband outside. He knew that we did not wish our fines to be paid, and was quite in sympathy with the militant campaign, but men are not so single-minded as women are; they are too much given to talking about their ideals, rather than *working* for them.

Even as socialites they seldom translate their faith into works, being still conservatives at heart, especially where women are concerned. Most of us who were married found that 'Votes for Women' were of less interest to our husbands than their own dinner. They simply could not understand why we made such a fuss about it.

1
The Struggle Begins

For most of history, the right to vote has been linked to the ownership of property; if you did not own land, you could not vote. This automatically ruled out all married women; everything that a married couple owned was legally the property of the husband! A very small number of women who were single or widows did own land, and it was a grey area as to whether they could vote. The long march to equality can be said to have arisen from the Reform Act of 1832. This extended the range of men who could vote, increasing the male electorate to about 20 per cent of the adult male population, but made no provision at all for any women to vote, not even those who owned land. Women began to organise themselves; the Sheffield Association for Female Suffrage was formed in 1851 and produced a suffrage petition which was presented to the House of Lords, and in the same year Harriet Taylor Mill published 'The Enfranchisement of Women' in the *Westminster Review*. Other groups soon followed. The Ladies' Institute at Langham Place was founded in 1857, starting a magazine, *The English Woman's Journal* (later *The Englishwomen's Review*) in the following year. In 1865, the Kensington Ladies' Discussion Society was founded, and, after Barbara Leigh Smith

Bodichon led a discussion on women's suffrage, a women's suffrage committee was formed. In 1867, societies promoting women's suffrage were formed in London, Manchester and Edinburgh. Bristol and Birmingham followed in 1868; the campaign was underway!

In practical terms, the only way to obtain the franchise was to persuade the all-male members of the House of Commons to vote for it. An individual MP might put forward a Bill to give women the vote, but it was the Government who controlled the timetable in the House of Commons; they might not allow enough time for a Bill of which they disapproved to pass through all the necessary stages to become law. Women really needed to persuade the Cabinet of their case, as they could not only allow the time for debate, but also urge the supporters of the Government to vote for it. It was these two all-male groupings, MPs in general and Cabinet ministers in particular, who had to be persuaded. The recognised way to make a change was by a petition, and the suffrage movement is often said to have really begun with that of 1867 which had 1,499 signatures, including such illustrious names as Harriet Martineau and Florence Nightingale; it was presented to John Stuart Mill, one of the small number of Members of Parliament already dedicated to the cause. There were to be many more petitions before women turned to other ways of making themselves heard.

The struggle for the vote was only one of many fields in which women were seeking respect. Others included the fields of education and medicine. There is a tradition that in 1855 Millicent Garrett and her sister Elizabeth were visited by Emily Davies at the Garrett family home in Aldeburgh in Suffolk; Emily and Elizabeth were about twenty years old, Millicent just eight. Emily is supposed to have said, 'It is clear enough what is to be done; you, Elizabeth, must open the medical profession to women, I must see about higher education, and as the vote will follow after the other two, Milly here, who is younger than we, must attend to that.' This is indeed what happened; Emily Davies became the founder of the first Cambridge college for women, and Elizabeth Garrett (later Anderson), the first British woman doctor. Millicent, under her married name of Millicent Fawcett, was one of the great leaders of the campaign to win the vote for women, as we shall see.

The whole question of the rights of married women was also a vital issue. According to the law, a married woman could not have any possessions of her own, everything was possessed by her husband. Once, Millicent Fawcett had her handbag snatched at Waterloo station. When she reported the incident to the station police, they recorded it not as the theft of one handbag, the property of Millicent Fawcett, but as the theft of one handbag, the property of Henry Fawcett (her husband)! It was this farcical situation that Millicent devoted her life to changing.

Further Acts of Parliament extended the franchise (the right to vote) to a growing number of men. In 1867 came the Second Reform Act; this increased the male electorate to approximately one-third of the adult male population. John Stuart Mill proposed to amend the Reform Act by replacing the word 'man' with 'person' so that women would also be covered by the Act; his amendment was defeated by a majority of 123. In the same year, one woman did vote for her Member of Parliament! After her accidental inclusion in the voting register, Lily Maxwell voted for Jacob Bright in a Parliamentary by-election in Manchester. This led to a legal test case, in 1869, which laid down that women could *not* take part in the election of members of Parliament.

Many men, and some women, instinctively felt that women should not be given the right to vote. In 1870, at a conference in Brighton, Millicent Garrett summed up a dozen arguments that people put against giving the vote to women:

1. Women are sufficiently represented already by men, and their interests have always been jealously protected by the legislature.

2. A woman is so easily influenced that if she had a vote it would have the same effect as giving two votes to her nearest male relation, or to her favourite clergyman.

3. Women are so obstinate that if they had votes, endless family discord would ensue.

4. The ideal of domestic life is a miniature despotism. One supreme head, to whom all other members of the family are subject. This ideal would be destroyed if the equality of women with men were recognised by extending the suffrage to women.

5. Women do not want the franchise.

6. The family is woman's proper sphere, and if she entered into politics she would be withdrawn from domestic duties.

7. The line must be drawn somewhere, and if women had

votes they would soon be wanting to enter the House of Commons.

8. Most women are Conservatives, and, therefore, their enfranchisement would have a reactionary influence on politics.

9. The indulgence and courtesy with which women are now treated by men would cease if women exercised all the rights and privileges of citizenship. Women would, therefore, on the whole, be losers, if they obtained the franchise.

10. The keen and intense excitement kindled by political strife would, if shared by women, deteriorate their physical powers, and would probably lead to the insanity of considerable numbers of them.

11. The exercise of political power by women is repugnant to the feelings and quite at variance with a due sense of propriety.

12. The notion that women have any claims to representation is so monstrous and absurd that no reasonable being would ever give the subject a moment's consideration.

These were the arguments that women were to be up against for the next half-century.

Local Government

In the last thirty years of the century, women did advance dramatically in terms of local government. In 1870, 2,000 School Boards were set up in England and Wales to provide schools for all children for the first time. It was extended to Scotland in 1872. These boards were elected; women could vote in these elections – and they could be candidates, whether they were married or not. In England and Wales, eleven women were elected at the very first elections in 1870, with a higher proportion in Scotland. In London, the first two women elected were Elizabeth Garrett and Emily Davies. There were about 370 women on the School Boards by 1902, but in that year they were abolished and their responsibilities taken over by borough and county councils – on which women could not sit as we shall see. Many women who cut their teeth on School Boards later became important figures in the suffrage campaign, most notably Emmeline Pankhurst, who was elected to the Manchester Board in 1900. Others included Isabella Ford in Leeds, Hannah Mitchell in Ashton and Charlotte Despard in London.

Boards of Guardians were established under the New Poor Law of 1834. They administered the poor rate and set up workhouses for the poor and unemployed. There was a property qualification, but it was uncertain whether women who did have property could be on these boards. This was accepted by the 1870s; the first woman elected was Martha Merrington at Kensington in 1875. There were eight women on Boards of Guardians by 1880, and eighty a decade later. The numbers increased after the abolition of the property qualification in 1894; there were about 900 women on Boards of Guardians by 1895.

A society to promote the return of women as Poor Law Guardians was founded in 1882. It gave nine reasons for having women as Guardians:

1. Because the larger number of paupers are women and children.

2. Because the great evil of Pauperism can only be diminished by more care in the bringing up of children.

3. Because the girls brought up in Pauper Schools require the superintendence of ladies to ensure their better training for domestic work.

4. Because experience has shown their utility in the Unions where Ladies have been elected as Poor Law Guardians.

5. Because so many women are ratepayers that they should be represented by women as well as men.

6. Because ladies are accustomed to visit among the poor, and are well acquainted with their requirements.

7. Because ladies have leisure and can give careful attention to matters brought before the Boards of Guardians.

8. Because many of the women who are brought before Guardians ought to be dealt with only by their own sex.

9. Because ladies, being accustomed to household management, are certain to exercise rigid economy in details.

It could be argued that these fields were the special concern of women, because they involved children. However, they were followed twenty years later by the spread of the right of women to vote in local elections. In 1885, Helen Taylor, a member of the Langham Place group, tried to put herself forward as a Parliamentary candidate for North Camberwell; her nomination papers were rejected by the returning officer. She was thirty years ahead of her time, but at a more local level women were getting elected into positions of authority.

County councils were founded in 1888; women ratepayers could vote, but it was not clear if they could be candidates for office. Parish councils and district councils were founded under an Act of 1894. Women ratepayers could vote, and any woman, married or single, ratepayer or resident, could stand for election. There were about 7,000 parish councils in England and Wales and somewhere between 80 and 200 women were elected at the first election. In Norfolk, for example, there were about twenty, though rarely more than one on any council; the little village of Stibbard led the way with no less than three of the original eight council members being women – a proportion achieved on very few governing bodies even today. The elected women included Mrs Harriet McIlquham, who had fought unsuccessfully for Cheltenham in county council elections in 1888, and then became chairman of Staverton Parish Council, Mrs Barker at Sherfield-on-Loddon, Hampshire, Mrs Forder at Guider Morden in Cambridgeshire, and Jane Escomb of Penshurst in Kent.

By 1907, there were over 2,000 women on parish and district councils and Poor Law Boards. In that year, the right was established for women to vote in county and borough councils. Outside London, seventeen women stood in the November 1907 city and borough council elections, five being successful; Elizabeth Garrett Anderson for Aldeburgh, Edith Sutton in Reading, Elizabeth Woodward for Bewdly near Kidderminster, Sophia Merivale in Oxford and Miss Dove in Wycombe. Aldeburgh and Bewdly were tiny boroughs, but the others were major towns with important councils. Including London, there were twenty-two women on these councils in 1910, doubling before war broke out in 1914 and elections were suspended for the duration.

London was a special case. Jane Cobden and Margaret, Lady Sandhurst, were elected to the London County Council in 1889, and Emma Cons was nominated as an alderman, with a life-long place on the council. Lady Sandhurst was unseated after a legal challenge by her male opponent, Beresford Hope; the other two were allowed to see out their terms but could not stand again. Other women served on London vestries from 1894.

Stimulated by these advances in local government, the campaign for the right to vote for Parliament moved forward. During the 1884 Reform Bill, William Woodall, Liberal MP for Stoke-on-Trent, proposed an amendment that any words importing the masculine gender should include women. He was supported by a letter signed by seventy-six representative women which was sent to every MP in the country:

We respectfully represent that the claim of duly qualified women for admission within the pale of the constitution is fully as pressing as that of the agricultural labourer, and that the body of electors who would thereby be added to the constituencies would be at least equal in general and political intelligence to the great body of agricultural and other labourers who are to be enfranchised by the Government Bill.

Among this body would be found women landowners, who form one-seventh of the land proprietors of the country; women of means and position living on their own property;

schoolmistresses and other teachers; women engaged in professional, literary, and artistic pursuits; women farmers, merchants, manufacturers, and shopkeepers; besides large numbers of self-supporting women engaged in industrial occupations. The continued exclusion of so large a proportion of the property, industry, and intelligence of the country from all representation in the Legislature is injurious to those excluded, and to the community at large.

Several Bills having special reference to the interests and status of women have been introduced in Parliament during the present session. This affords a powerful reason for the immediate enfranchisement of women, in order that members of Parliament may have the same sense of responsibility towards the class affected by them as in dealing with questions relating to men.

Gladstone, as Prime Minister, opposed the granting of the vote to women, and many MPs known to be friends of women's suffrage followed his lead; a women's suffrage journal calculated that if all these MPs had voted according to their convictions, the clause would have been easily carried.

The main weapon that the groups used was still the petition; almost every year, a petition signed by men and women urging Parliament to grant women the right to vote was sent in to the House of Commons. Petitions had been a traditional form of protest for many centuries: large numbers were organised, many by women, during the successful campaign to abolish slavery almost a century before. Women's suffrage petitions presented to the House of Commons totalled 61,475 names in 1869, rising to 430,343 in 1874 and then falling, before a return to the high levels in the 1890s.

In 1892, a Bill to extend the Parliamentary franchise to women on local government registers was defeated by just fifteen votes. It led to a petition from women, which by the time it was presented in 1894, had 248,000 signatures; the Report of the Appeal Committee noted that

> the signatures included the heads of nearly all the colleges for women and of a large proportion of the head mistresses of High and other Public Schools for girls, and of women serving on Boards of Guardians and School Boards. The leading women in the medical profession signed, and a number of the most eminent in literature and art, besides many of wide social influence, and many leading workers in the various movements for general well-being.

By 1896, when it was shown in Westminster Hall, the number had risen to 257,796. A Glasgow MP named Faithfull Begg put forward a Bill in that year, and another in 1897. The 1896 Bill ran out of time. The 1897 Bill passed its second reading by a majority of 71, but in committee its opponents spent so much time discussing other matters that there was no time to discuss this one, and time again ran out.

It was not only women in professions who felt that they ought to have the vote. In 1901, a petition from 29,000 women working in mills in Lancashire was brought to London by a deputation of fifteen working women and given in to the House of Commons. Women in mills in Lancashire and Yorkshire were very strong in their demand for the vote; Annie Kenney, who had started working part-time in a Lancashire cotton mill at the age of ten, was to become one of the leaders of the suffragette movement.

2
1900–1906

By the beginning of the twentieth century, there were a few women in professions such as medicine, a few going to University, and quite a large number working on Boards of Guardians, School Boards and parish councils. However, no woman could even vote for their Member of Parliament, let alone think of becoming an MP. It was time for stronger action. The campaign for the women's vote was one dear to the heart of many women, but it did not produce a single unified movement. There were an enormous number of societies and groups promoting the cause, two or three of which played the leading role.

The first was the National Union of Women's Suffrage Societies (NUWSS), founded in 1897 by Millicent Fawcett, whom we have already mentioned; its members were known as suffragists. It was an umbrella group at first, co-ordinating the activities of the many local societies and aiming to publicise their cause. As one member, Mrs Thomas Taylor, pointed out, 'there are hundreds and thousands of women who do care for the suffrage; but there are millions – I speak advisedly – millions who not only do not care, but who have, many of them, never heard of it, and certainly do not realise what it means'. The suffragists of the society would spread the word so that 'no one in future will be able to say that they have not heard of woman suffrage; and no one will be able to think, or to pretend they think, that the suffrage means that every woman will try for a seat in Parliament, or that it will lead to every man having as many wives as the Mormons, or to every woman having three husbands, as in Thibet'. By 1906, it had become an active centralised organisation.

In 1903, a 'rival' group, the Women's Social and Political Union (WSPU) was founded in Manchester by Emmeline Pankhurst and her daughters Christabel, Sylvia and Adela; they thought the already-existing group was too feeble, and also too middle-class. They were to become a *militant* group, but this word needs to be placed in the context of its time. The militant acts of extremist groups in the later twentieth century are a world apart from those of the suffragettes. Their 'militancy' consisted at first of shouting down politicians, and of marches which often involved confrontation with the police. The Pankhursts led by the sheer force of their personalities. Rebecca West wrote of Emmeline's oratory, 'Trembling like a reed, she lifted up her hoarse, sweet voice on the platform, but the reed was of steel, and it was tremendous.' Max Beerbohm was entranced by Christabel when he saw her in court: 'Her whole body is alive with her every meaning ... imagine a very graceful, rhythmic dance done by a dancer who does not move her feet.'

Always the smaller group, the activities of the WSPU made women think about the suffrage issue and thus helped the NUWSS gain membership; there were only sixteen societies within it in 1903, but over 400 just ten years later. It also made people willing to dedicate their whole lives to the cause – one of the NUWSS leaders, Ray Strachey, talks of an 'almost religious fervour'.

The Manchester Free Trade Hall, 13 October 1905

Emmeline Pankhurst herself dated the start of militancy from an impromptu protest she organised on 12 May 1905 after a women's suffrage Bill had been talked out of Parliament. However, it was on 13 October 1905 that the group thrust itself into the public view. Christabel Pankhurst and Annie Kenney went to a meeting in Manchester Free Trade Hall held by Cabinet minister Sir Edward Grey. They displayed a small home-made banner that read, 'VOTES FOR WOMEN'. On being thrown out of the hall, they became involved in a confrontation outside with the police. They were arrested and fined 10 shillings and 5 shillings respectively. They refused to pay and were sent to Strangeways Prison. For the first time, women had been imprisoned for their campaign for the right to vote. It was also the first occasion a Cabinet minister had been targeted for harassment: this became a typical tactic of the WSPU from this date onwards.

Millicent Fawcett saw that the significance of this new development lay in the publicity that it gave to the movement. She later wrote,

> We had become quite accustomed to holding magnificent meetings in support of women's franchise with every evidence of public support, and to receive from the anti-suffrage press

either no notice at all or only a small paragraph tucked away in an inconspicuous corner. The sensation caused by the action of the WSPU suddenly changed all this. Instead of the withering contempt of silence, the Anti-Suffrage papers came out day after day with columns of hysterical verbiage directed against our movement ... if abuse and misrepresentation could have killed it, it most assuredly would have died in the early years of the twentieth century.

Like campaigners for other causes later in the century, many women would have argued that any kind of publicity was ultimately good for the cause, as long as it kept the campaign in the public eye; but, to remain in the public eye, the acts of protest would have to become evermore extreme.

Although women could not vote or stand in Parliamentary elections, they could try and make themselves heard. There was a general election in January 1906. Just one candidate in the election specifically ran as a women's suffrage candidate, Thorley Smith at Wigan; his expenses were paid by the Lancashire and Cheshire Women Textile and Other Workers' Representation Committee: Dora Montefiore was one of those who supported his campaign. He came second, 1,300 votes behind the winning Conservative; 2,205 men had given him their vote. These numbers sound small compared to votes in elections today, because relatively few people had the right to vote. The WSPU targeted Winston Churchill, not because they had anything particularly against him, but because he was the most important figure in the Manchester area. The Liberals won the general election. The Prime Minister was Sir Henry Campbell Bannerman, who was personally in favour of women's suffrage; however, many of his Cabinet ministers were against it.

Meanwhile, the WSPU were going from strength to strength. In February, Emmeline Pethick-Lawrence joined the movement; she and Mrs Pankhurst – 'the two Emmelines' – were to lead it over the next five years. Emmeline Pethick-Lawrence's husband, Fred, a lawyer, also played an important part in the movement. The WSPU held its first large London meeting at Caxton Hall in the same month, concluding with a deputation of women to the House of Commons; they found the doors of the Strangers' Entrance closed to them.

It was at this time that the word 'suffragette' came into existence; it was coined by the *Daily Mail*, first appearing in the paper on 10 January 1906. It was one of those words, like 'Tory' or Quaker', intended as criticism but taken up by those it was aimed against. It was used to suggest a person who was prepared to go beyond the law to further the cause, in contrast to the 'suffragist' who kept to legal forms of protest. The distinction between the two words was not always strictly observed, however, either at the time or in more recent accounts.

The first of the great women's deputations came three months later, on 19 May 1906. Organised by the NUWSS, twenty-six organisations were represented – including the WSPU. More than 300 people met Campbell-Bannerman. He told them that he was personally in favour, but that he could do nothing because of opposition of the other leaders within his own party – his advice was 'to go on pestering'.

Direct action by the WSPU took place in the following month. On 19 June, Teresa Billington, Annie Kenney and two working women were arrested for disorderly conduct, arising out of a disturbance when they had attempted to call on Asquith after his refusal to receive a deputation. They were sixty-four-year-old Jane Sbarboro, the wife of an Italian workman resident in East London, and Adelaide Knight, severely disabled since childhood. Teresa Billington refused to acknowledge the authority of the court to try women. She was fined £10 with the alternative of two months in prison – the fine was not paid and she was taken to Holloway, the first women's rights campaigner to go to the London gaol that became increasingly associated with their cause. The sentence was halved, and she did not even serve that as an anonymous reader of the *Daily Mirror* paid her fine; in a reversal of the usual situation, she was ordered to leave the prison!

As a lawyer, Pethick-Lawrence was asked by his wife to help defend the other three. Asked at her trial why she had been involved in the demonstration, Adelaide Knight answered, 'Because we want the vote. We see the misery you men have done over the years and we want to alter it … You would have sympathy if you lived down Bow Common and saw the misery there. I think women can undo the tangle you men have made.' They were bound over to keep the peace; however, they refused on principle and were sent to prison for six weeks. Some papers referred to them as 'martyrettes'. They were released on 14 August.

In September, the WSPU moved its base of operations to London, opening official headquarters at Clement's Inn.

In the process, the group became much more middle-class. Alice Milne, a working-class member from Manchester visited the new HQ in London – 'If our Adult Suffrage Socialist friend could have looked in that room, he would have said more than ever that ours was a movement for the middle and upper classes. What a fever our Union members in Manchester would have been in if such ladies made a descent on us.'

Further action came almost at once. Parliament opened on 23 October; Mrs Pethick-Lawrence and other WSPU members staged a demonstration in the House of Commons. Thrown out, she tried to get back in and was arrested. She and ten others, including Annie Cobden Sanderson, Sylvia and Adela Pankhurst, Mary Gawthorpe, Edith How Martyn, Dora Montefiore and Irene Miller, were bound to keep peace for six months. They refused, so were committed to prison for two months 'in the second division' and sent to Holloway. The 'division' relates to the severity of the conditions in which prisoners were kept; the second division was for 'common criminals'. First division was for very minor crimes (misdemeanours) and prisoners had a number of privileges – wearing their own clothes, reading books and newspapers, visiting with friends. In the second (and third) divisions, prisoners had to wear prison uniforms, were kept in solitary confinement for all but one hour a day, and were allowed no visitors or letters. Several of the women broke down in prison and were released, while the Home Secretary transferred the others from the second to the first division, a significant move as it meant that they were being recognised as political prisoners rather than just criminals.

Anne Cobden Sanderson was a high-profile figure who brought the campaign much publicity; she was the daughter of the radical politician Richard Cobden. The playwright George Bernard Shaw wrote to *The Times*, complaining of 'one of the nicest women in England suffering from the coarsest indignity'.

The NUWSS, like many of the public and a large part of the House of Commons, was shocked that the women should be sent to Holloway as common criminals, and thought the punishment harsh and excessive for what they had done. Millicent Fawcett publicly announced her support for the prisoners and urged her fellow suffragists to stand by them:

> The real responsibility for these sensational methods lies with the politicians, misnamed statesmen, who will not attend to a demand for justice until it is accompanied by some form of violence. Every kind of insult and abuse is hurled at the women who have adopted these methods, especially by the 'reptile' press. But I hope the more old-fashioned suffragists will stand by them; and I take this opportunity of saying that in my opinion, far from having injured the movement, they have done more during the last twelve months to bring it within the region of practical politics than we have been able to accomplish in the same number of years.

In a letter that Fawcett wrote to friends she added, 'I feel that the action of the prisoners has touched the imagination of the country in a manner which quieter methods did not succeed in doing.' The WSPU responded warmly to Fawcett's expressions of support. Emmeline Pethick-Lawrence, the treasurer, called Fawcett's action 'a generous and noble gesture', and Elizabeth Robins, a member of the executive committee of the WSPU, thanked her effusively for her support:

> They are grateful to you – these women who are fighting the much-misunderstood battle in the open. Some of them know quite well they would stand a poor chance indeed, but for the past influence and present championship of yourself and others like you – if there are others … The generous attitude of one like yourself must be of invaluable help to those of us who cannot hope to ever to be so well equipped, and yet have come to feel they must not hold back one voice through an ignoble fear of the bugbear charge of notoriety-hunting.

The NUWSS held a banquet in honour of the prisoners on 11 December 1906, after their release from Holloway.

There would not be another general election for four years, but there were several by-elections each year as MPs died or retired. All the newspapers carried detailed reports of these campaigns, providing opportunities for publicity for the cause. Women's groups would hold meetings, urge voters to think about the issue of female suffrage, and most of them encouraged men to vote for the candidate most likely to support it. The WSPU had a more subtle policy, always campaigning against the Liberal candidate on the grounds that it was the Liberal Government which was denying them the vote. The first by-election in which the WSPU were involved was at Cockermouth in August 1906. Christabel Pankhurst hired a stall in the marketplace and sold 'Votes for Women' literature. When a crowd had gathered, she stood on a stool and addressed them, urging them to vote against the Liberal candidate in order to show the Government that they did not approve of its refusal to give votes to women. She was joined in the campaign by other suffragettes, and the Liberal was indeed defeated.

Hannah Mitchell was in Huddersfield for the by-election there in November:

With all her ablest lieutenants in prison, Mrs Pankhurst asked me to go there with her to open a campaign against the Government. It was difficult for me to leave home just then, but I went with her. On the night of our arrival we two alone held a meeting at the market cross which roused so much interest that at the close we had enough volunteers to bill the town the next day [she means, to cover the town with posters and leaflets]. Presently women began to arrive from all parts – Mrs Martel from London, Mrs Coates-Hanson from Middlesbrough, Mrs Baines from Stockport, Alice Milne from Manchester – to offer help in the campaign. Hundreds of women would attend afternoon meetings, and walk round the town in procession afterwards, pausing outside the Liberal committee rooms to raise the cry, 'Vote against the Government.' Huge posters asked in bold letters: 'Why is Cobden's daughter in prison?' We so beset and bedevilled the Liberal candidate that the Government gave in, and released all the prisoners half way through their sentences. They took the first train to Huddersfield, where we had booked all the available halls, which were packed long before the train was due. I was holding the fort in a large hall which became so packed that I had to engage another room for an overflow meeting. Helen Fraser, a Scotswoman, whom we called the chieftainess because of her fine presence and air of command, was with me, and we talked to the women – we were beyond speeches – until some of the ex-prisoners came along. Huddersfield honoured itself that day by the welcome it gave those women. Yet not one of those three candidates had the manliness to declare himself openly on our side ... The Liberal won the seat with a reduced majority. All three candidates are dead now and forgotten, but Huddersfield still remembers the Suffragettes.

Almost all Members of Parliament were Liberals or Conservatives, with a sizeable number of Irish Nationalists. The 1906 general election saw the emergence of a new party, the Labour Party. It had just thirty MPs at first but its leader, James Keir Hardie, was a fervent supporter of the cause of 'Votes For Women'. He introduced a women's suffrage resolution in Parliament in April 1906. He said that the present unrest was a result of the deputation to the Prime Minister; Campbell-Bannerman had told the women that no Bill would come before the present Parliament. Keir Hardie claimed that 420 MPs were pledged to women's suffrage, so that if a Bill were introduced it would certainly be passed. Another supporter was the Irish MP Willie Redmond. He said he wanted women to have the vote because he was opposed to slavery in any form: 'Any of God's creatures who are denied a voice in the Government of their country are more or less slaves ... Men have no right to assume that they are so superior to women that they alone have the right to govern.' Suffragettes in the Ladies' Gallery protested as other Members, especially a Mr Cremer, ridiculed the measure, which was talked out, no time being allowed for a vote on the issue.

3
1907: Marches and By-Elections

February 1907 saw the protest march taken to a new level, with the first of the great NUWSS processions in London, from Trafalgar Square to Exeter Hall. Between 3,000 and 4,000 women took part in what became known as 'the mud march' because it took place during a downpour. It is hard now to imagine what a bold step going on a march was for these women. As Ray Strachey recalled, 'In that year the vast majority of women still felt that there was something very dreadful in walking in procession through the streets; to do it was to be something of a martyr, and many of the demonstrators felt that they were risking their employments and endangering their reputations, besides facing a dreadful ordeal of ridicule and public shame.' There was no violence, and similar marches soon followed elsewhere in the country. Many of the marchers were women who had achieved much in life, such as Ethel Williams, born in Cromer in Norfolk, who had become the first female doctor in Newcastle.

The WSPU also became increasingly active. In February, a convention calling itself a 'Women's Parliament' met at Caxton Hall in London. About 800 women marched to the Houses of Parliament, where they were involved in violent confrontations with mounted police. The event gave the

WSPU an enormous amount of publicity. In the Commons on the next day a Mr Hay protested at the police violence, commenting, 'Women had rights as well as men.' Keir Hardie said that an eyewitness had told him that excessive violence had been used, but the Home Secretary, Herbert Gladstone, said that he had no reason to suppose that this was the case. Fifty-seven women and two men were charged after the events; they included Christabel and Sylvia Pankhurst and Charlotte Despard. Charlotte was born Charlotte French; her brother was Sir John French, one of the most important figures in the British army. She was a wealthy widow, and destined to become a key figure in the struggle.

On 9 March, a private member's Bill to give votes to women was introduced by W. H. Dickinson but talked out – this time seventy-two were arrested in the subsequent protest. One MP, Mr Massie, said it was a step forward that the debate was conducted free of 'the joke and gibe' that accompanied previous debates. He then proceeded to disparage the women's case; his argument was one commonly used at the time, that Government ultimately depended upon force – the police and the armed forces. As women could not serve in these forces, they could never hold ultimate power. As for the textile workers from Northern towns, they only wanted the vote, he claimed, because they had been told that it would increase their wages.

Public meetings helped publicise the campaign, put the case to the public – and raise money. Hannah Mitchell recalled,

In May [1907] I think, I was asked to go to London to speak at the several meetings, one of which was in Exeter Hall. There the enthusiasm of the large audience was so great that the collection realised 1,100 pounds. Then women began to take off their jewellery, and send it up the platform to be sold for 'The Cause'. I am not suggesting that my speech roused all this fire, although I received many compliments on it. Some of the finest speakers in England were on the platform that night, and I was proud to be thought worthy of a place among them.

Another night I was sent to Kensington Town Hall where I was told there was a special request for a working woman speaker from Lancashire. Our good friend H. W. Nevinson [a journalist and one of the men who were committed to the cause] was in the chair. I was not often nervous, but that audience seemed more formidable than the Northern roughs. Men and women in evening dress filled the hall; rich gowns and flashing diamonds met the eye everywhere. Among those on the platform was Violet Hunt, the writer, in an evening gown with roses in her hair; others were similarly attired, and there was I, in a little black frock I had made myself. I never had any jewellery, but my hostess, Mrs Cullen, had given me a little paste buckle on black velvet for my neck, and had herself arranged my hair in a thick plait like a coronet, so I daresay I did not actually offend the eye, and as always my nervousness vanished when I rose to speak.

The WSPU held more than 5,000 meetings in 1907 and 1908, many very well attended; 400 of these meetings each drew more than 1,000 people!

By-elections continued to occupy a great deal of women's energy, and in May 1907 one was fought with a candidate specifically urging the right of women to the vote. This was the philosopher Bertrand Russell, who would go on to become a famous protester again half a century later in the Campaign for Nuclear Disarmament. In 1907 he stood for parliament at a by-election at Wimbledon on behalf of votes for women, sponsored by the NUWSS; this was the first time they had done this. The only other candidate was a Conservative, Sir Henry Chaplin, who was an outspoken opponent of women's suffrage. Russell recalled in his *Autobiography*,

The Wimbledon Campaign was short and arduous. It must be quite impossible for younger people to imagine the bitterness of the opposition to women's equality. When, in later years, I campaigned against the First World War, the popular opposition that I encountered was not comparable to that which the suffragists met in 1907. The whole subject was treated, by a great majority of the population, as one for mere hilarity. The crowd would shout derisive remarks: to women, 'Go home and mind the baby'; to men, 'Does your mother know you're out?' no matter what the man's age. Rotten eggs were aimed at me and hit my wife. At my first meeting rats were let loose to frighten the ladies, and ladies who were in the plot screamed in pretended terror with a view to disgracing their sex ... The savagery of the males who were threatened with loss of supremacy was intelligible. But the determination of large numbers of women to prolong the contempt of the female sex was odd. I cannot recall any violent agitation of negroes or Russian serfs against emancipation.

However, Sylvia Pankhurst thought that Russell had fought the campaign as a Liberal rather than primarily as a women's suffrage candidate; as Wimbledon was a naturally Conservative seat he was heavily defeated – but, she claimed, this had nothing to do with the popularity or otherwise of the women's cause.

There was a further split in suffragette ranks in September 1907, when Emmeline Pankhurst formed what she called the National WSPU, whose members had to sign a pledge not to support *any* party at parliamentary elections until women had obtained the vote. Those members who wanted to work with the Labour Party had to leave; a group of women broke away to form the Women's Freedom League (WFL). This, naturally, tended to take in the working-class women, so that, in practice, the National WSPU became even more a middle-class organisation. Leading figures in the WFL movement included Charlotte Despard, Teresa Billington-Greig (she had married Frederick Greig), Edith How Martyn and Anne Cobden Sanderson. They thought that violent militancy was working against the cause and making it unlikely that any Bill would be passed; militancy in the form of passive resistance rather than violence would impress both the public and Parliament. Charlotte Despard even discussed these matters with Gandhi, the great exponent of the principle of passive resistance.

The WFL was the smallest of the three main suffrage groups, but it had a lot of influence. It had a strong presence in Scotland, where many of its meetings were organised by Anna Munro, noted for her oratory, and Janet (Jenny) McCallum. One of its main speakers in Wales was Emily Phipps, headteacher at Swansea higher grade school. She and a friend, Clare Neal, joined the WFL in 1908 after hearing an anti-suffrage speech by Lloyd George in the city.

Emmeline thought that the autocratic organisational structure of the WSPU was the most effective structure for winning the vote. As she emphasised, 'the WSPU is not hampered by a complexity of rules. We have no constitutional and by-laws; nothing to be amended or tinkered with or quarrelled over at an annual meeting. In fact, we have no annual meeting, no business sessions, no elections of officer. The WSPU is simply a suffrage army in the field. It is purely a volunteer army, and no one is obliged to remain in it.' In reality, as Rebecca West was to comment in 1933, in the midst of her battle for democracy, Emmeline Pankhurst was obliged, lest that battle should be lost, to become a dictator. In practice, however, the WSPU was run by the Pethick-Lawrences and Christabel Pankhurst, who became known as 'The Triumvirate'. Emmeline instead embarked on a never-ending tour of meetings, speeches and by-election campaigns. Mabel Tuke became honorary secretary of the National WSPU, a post she was to hold for eight years, and Cicely Hale, a secretary by profession, organised the information. Elizabeth Robins became a committee member; she was an actress and playwright. Her play *Votes for Women*, performed in 1907, was the first example of suffrage drama.

Alice Kenney reinforced the comparison of being in the WSPU with serving in an army,

> Nuns in a convent were not watched over and supervised more strictly than were the organisers and members of the Militant Movement during the first few years. It was an unwritten rule that there must be no concerts, no theatres, no smoking; work and sleep to prepare us for more work, was the unwritten order of the day. These rules were good, and the more I look back on those early days the more clearly I see the need for such discipline. The changed life into which most of us entered was a revolution in itself. No home-life, no one to say what we should or should not do, no family ties, we were free and alone in a great brilliant city, scores of young women scarcely out of their teens met together in a revolutionary movement, outlaws or breakers of laws, independent of everything and everybody, fearless and self-confident.

In October, the Pethick-Lawrences brought out the first number of *Votes for Women*. It began as a monthly paper but soon became a weekly, selling at 1*d*. At its peak it was selling over 30,000 copies a week. When the Pethick-Lawrences were in prison, the paper was edited by Evelyn Sharp. The NUWSS followed suit two years later with a paper called *The Common Cause*, edited from 1909 to 1912 by Helena Swanwick. Many of the leading stores advertised in these publications, often with half- or full-page advertisements. They included Debenham & Freebody, Swan & Edgar, Burberry's, and Marshall & Snelgrove.

Some were geared specifically to the suffragette audience, offering products like a suffragette coat in purple and green, or underwear in white, green and purple. The paper carried articles urging its readers to patronise its advertisers – 'these firms are helping us to fight the battle, and you are helping by patronising them'. In the issue for 27 January 1911, for example, the paper recommended thirty-seven shops and twenty well-known products – including Colman's Mustard! In some circles a suffragette look was becoming distinctly fashionable; many supporters enjoyed challenging the assumption that all suffragettes were frumps who dressed appallingly. This could help the cause; when Gladice Keevil gave a speech in Leeds, the local newspaper described her as 'a young lady with a winning smile and a most becoming hat'. The advertisements were aimed directly at the wealthy suffragette; they invited readers to shop at the exclusive Derry & Toms, or, on one occasion, to buy fur coats that cost around 195 guineas; eight years' earnings on a working woman's wage! Many wealthy people gave financial support to the movement, such as Clara Mordan, who had inherited a fortune from her father, a maker of propelling pencils. She suffered from tuberculosis, so her contribution was financial rather than physical; she gave at least £1,500 to the WSPU in the seven years after 1906. When Emmeline Pankhurst was released from prison in January 1909, Clara presented her with an amethyst, pearl and emerald necklace.

4

1908: New Tactics

January 1908 saw a new tactic, and one with which many people still think of when they think about the suffragette movement: the act of chaining oneself to railings in protest. On 17 January, the Cabinet council met at 10 Downing Street to draw up the future Parliamentary programme. Suffragettes gathered outside. Two of them, Edith New and Olivia Smith, had brought heavy steel chains and padlocks; they ran to the railings outside Number 10, and fastened themselves to them, calling out for 'Votes for Women'. The police had to break the chains, and, while this was happening, two other women, Flora Drummond and Mary MacArthur, actually managed to get into the Prime Minister's house, where they were arrested. The authorities, in sentencing the women to imprisonment, reverted to placing them in the second division. Emmeline Pethick-Lawrence saw the significance of the act, writing in *Votes for Women*, 'Doing something silly is the women's alternative for doing something cruel. The effect is the same. We use no violence because we can win freedom for women without it; because we have discovered an alternative.'

Activity at by-elections reached a peak at the Mid Devon by-election in January 1908. The suffragettes supported the

Conservative candidate, who had an unexpected victory over
the Liberal. Although most of the press derided the work
of suffragettes in by-elections, the *Manchester Guardian*
thought differently:

> There can be no doubt that the Suffragists did influence votes.
> Their activity, the interest shown in their meetings, the success
> of their persuasive methods in enlisting popular sympathy,
> the large number of working women who acted with them
> as volunteers – these were features of the by-election which,
> although strangely ignored by most of the newspapers, must
> have struck most visitors to the constituency.

The by-election also showed the physical risks suffragettes
took in their campaign. Mary Gawthorpe had to push away
a man who tried to climb onto the wagon from which she
was speaking, and a few days later youths seized the lorry
from which suffragettes were speaking, and dragged it round
and round so violently it almost overturned; they stopped
only after a little boy had been run over and badly hurt.

When the result was announced, Emmeline Pankhurst
and her co-worker, Nellie Martel, were attacked by a group
of young male clay-cutters who had supported the ousted
Liberal candidate. Sylvia Pankhurst graphically describes
what happened:

> The roughs of Newton Abbot, the principal town in the
> constituency, were notorious. The banding of them into a
> 'League of Young Liberals' now cloaked their undisciplined
> savagery with the respectable mantle of politics. Their first

act of war was to push a policeman through the window of the Suffragette committee rooms. After the declaration of the poll, the successful Tory was escorted from the town by a strong force of police. The occupants of the Conservative Club were besieged by a noisy mob, and kept prisoners the whole night ... Mrs Pankhurst and Mrs Martel were the only suffragettes who remained for the declaration of the poll. Local people advised them to hasten away, but they ridiculed any suggestion of danger. They were set upon and beaten in the street. A woman shopkeeper succeeded in dragging Mrs Martel inside her shop for safety, but Mrs Pankhurst was left outside with the mob. She was thrown to the ground, and a barrel was brought to roll her in. The police appeared just in time to save her, but she had received an injury to her ankle which was a recurring source of pain and disability for many years.

Confronted by the mob, Emmeline did not lose her nerve, asking contemptuously, 'Are none of you *men*?' Although the mob fled when the police arrived, it was two hours before it was considered safe for the women to leave.

This degree of violence was unusual and some of the NUWSS were impressed with the campaigns of the WSPU, including Isabella Ford, who wrote to Mrs Fawcett about the South Leeds by-election of February 1908, at which Emmeline campaigned despite her injured ankle: 'The WSPU behaved splendidly – and there were no rows. I see more and more [that] their policy is far more workable than ours: but we never clashed. We only did propaganda work – I longed to "go for" the Liberal and had to hold myself down.'

The WSPU held a three-day session of its annual Women's Parliament in February, after which its supporters tried as usual to protest at the House of Commons. In the melee, Emmeline Pankhurst herself was arrested, along with several other women, and taken to Holloway Prison. She later described the experience:

Arriving at the prison we groped our way through dim corridors into the reception ward, where we were lined up against the wall for a superficial medical examination. After that we were locked in separate cells, unfurnished except for low wooden stools.

It seemed an endless time before my cell door was opened by a wardress, who ordered me to follow her. I entered a room where another wardress sat at a table, ready to take an inventory of my effects. Obeying an order to undress, I took off my gown, then paused. 'Take off everything' was the next order. 'Everything?' I faltered. It seemed impossible that they expected me to strip. In fact, they did allow me to take off my last garments in the shelter of a bath-room. I shivered myself into some frightful underclothing, old and patched and stained, some coarse brown woollen stockings with red stripes, and the hideous prison dress stamped all over with the broad arrow of disgrace. I fished a pair of shoes out of a big basket of shoes, old and mostly mismates. A pair of coarse but clean sheets, a towel, a mug of cold cocoa, and a thick slice of brown bread were given me, and I was conducted to my cell.

She wrote later,

The poor prisoner, when she entered Holloway, dropped, as it were, into a tomb. No letters and no visitors were allowed for the first month of the sentence. Think of it – a whole month, more than four weeks, without sending or receiving a single word. One's nearest and dearest may have gone through dreadful suffering, may have been ill, may have died, meantime. One was given plenty of time to imagine all these things, for the prisoner was kept in solitary confinement in a narrow, dimly-lit cell, twenty-three hours out of the twenty-four. Solitary confinement is too terrible a punishment to inflict on any human being, whatever his crime ... Picture what it must be to a woman who has committed some small offence, for most of the women who go to Holloway are small offenders, sitting alone, day after day, in the heavy silence of a cell – thinking of her children at home – thinking, thinking. Some women go mad. Many suffer from shattered nerves for a long period after release.

Emmeline never forgot the harshness and indignity of prison. After two days of solitary confinement, afflicted with migraines, she was sent to the hospital where she was awoken, during the night, by the moaning of a woman in the cell next to her own. She suddenly realised that the woman was in labour. 'I shall never forget that night,' she recollected, 'nor what I suffered with the birth-pangs of that woman, who, I found later, was simply waiting trial on a charge which was found to be baseless.'

Released on 19 March, Emmeline could have rested quietly, at home. Instead, she made an unexpected entrance at an Albert Hall meeting that night, to mark the end of a Self-Denial Week to raise money for the cause. Like an actress in the wings, she waited till all the others were seated and then walked quietly onto the stage, removed the placard on her seat saying 'Mrs Pankhurst's Chair' and sat down to great applause. Deeply moved by the love shown her, it was some time before she could speak: 'I for one, friends, looking around on the muddles that men have made, looking round on the sweated and decrepit members of my sex, I say men have had the control of these things long enough, and no woman with any spark of womanliness in her will consent to let this state of things go on any longer.' From 1908, the WSPU met at the Albert Hall every March, May and October, the meetings being always packed. Mrs Pankhurst appeared with Christabel Pankhurst and Emmeline Pethick Lawrence, until the historic meeting of October 1912 when she appeared alone.

While Mrs Pankhurst and her supporters were reaching Parliament in the ordinary way, another group had thought up a more outrageous approach. Twenty women, including Marie and Georgina Brackenbury and Elsie and Marie Howey, adopted a tactic based on that of the Trojan horse; they went to the House of Commons in a large horse-drawn van, of the kind then known as a pantechnicon. However, when they burst open the doors in front of the House of Commons, the police were ready for them, and they were taken to prison in a very different vehicle, police 'Black Marias'. The *Daily Mirror* noticed the 'new WSPU tactics. Among the methods which the Suffrage Movement has so far introduced into political warfare are: bell ringing – door knocking – police court protests – voluntary imprisonment

– chain and padlock tableaux – systematic minister baiting
– the pantechnicon – megaphone and taxi appeal.'

The Women's Suffrage Bill, 28 February 1908

During Mrs Pankhurst's time in prison, her dream of
women's suffrage had come closer to being a reality than
she might have hoped. A women's suffrage Bill, put forward
by Henry Stanger (Liberal MP for North Kensington),
passed a second reading by a majority of 179, marking
the first time since 1897 that the House of Commons had
acted favourably on a women's suffrage measure. The Bill
proposed that in all Acts relating to the qualification and
registration of voters, words appearing to refer only to men
should be held to include women – and also that a woman
should not be disqualified from being so registered to vote
merely because she was married.

The debate was heated. Charles Mallett, Liberal MP for
Plymouth, was an opponent; he disparaged the countries
that had already given the vote to women – Australia and
New Zealand were 'young colonies with their limited
political experience and their rather crude political
methods'. The four American states that allowed women to
vote were also criticised – Idaho and Wyoming 'comprised
mining camps and cattle ranches', Colorado was 'one of the
worst-governed states of the union' and Utah was described
by Mallett simply as 'the Mormon state'. Sir Walter Nugent,
Nationalist MP for West Meath, said that most women did
not want the vote: 'Why did they try to force upon them
what they did not want? Was it because a small and noisy

minority were making the days and nights of Cabinet ministers hideous with their howlings? ... It had been said that the result of the county council franchise had been for their benefit. In his experience, he had never met one who did not look upon it as a nuisance.'

Sir Maurice Levy, Liberal MP for Mid Leicestershire, drew attention to the undoubted status of many of the most active suffragettes: 'The promoters of the Bill who seemed to be a few rich women would be allowed to have a vote and a seat in Parliament which at the same time would be denied to the bulk of the working women of the country.' He also raised the spectre that, if they were allowed to vote, women would soon be wanting actually to become Members of Parliament! He drew attention to a letter by Gladstone to the late Samuel Smith:

> For a long time we drew a distinction between competency to vote and competency to sit in Parliament. But long before our electorate had attained to its present popular proportions this distinction was felt to involve a possible inconsistency, and accordingly it died away. It surely cannot be revived; and if it cannot be revived, then the woman's vote carries with it, whether by the same Bill, or by a consequential Bill, the woman's seat in Parliament ... Capacity to sit in the House of Commons now legally and practically draws in its train capacity to fill every office in the State.

Other members opposed the Bill for a very different reason: they wanted every adult, male or female, included in a Bill. One such speaker was Clement Edwards, Liberal

MP for Denbigh. He opposed the Bill because he was in favour of adult suffrage: 'He, for one, had not been in the least frightened by the boisterous and somewhat Olympic methods of the active crusaders whom he supposed they might correctly describe as belonging to the future vanguard of the suffrage movement.'

Stanger himself drew attention to what had been achieved by women already:

> We have only to look round to see the number of occupations, not domestic, some of them public or quasi-public in their character, now filled by women with credit and even with distinction. We have only to remember that in every other governing body except this – in all our local government arrangements – women cannot merely exercise the vote as freely as men, but are qualified to sit on these governing bodies ... In these municipalities enormous sums of money are spent, many of them are huge industrial concerns. Great questions have often been discussed, and yet woman is fully entitled not only to vote for representatives, but also to sit and deal with these matters.

Herbert Pike Pearse, Conservative MP for Darlington, was in favour *despite* the militants' campaign:

> An argument which has considerable effect in the country, though perhaps not so much in this House, is that ladies have recently shown that they can act in such a way as to make it impossible for the men of this country to grant the franchise. That is, that women's behaviour has been so bad in regard

to the riots which have taken place lately that we ought not on that account to pass any measure for the extension of the franchise to women. I think that, though we may not agree as to the methods that have been employed, we must all agree that the intensity of their feelings has been shown by the willingness of these women to endure hardship, and also that many of these ladies probably are very well qualified to act as voters in this country. It does not follow that the whole class of women should be prevented from voting simply because a certain number of ladies act in a violent manner. If that were so, then it would be possible to argue that if there were a thousand criminals in the male class in this country all the men should be disenfranchised.

Philip Snowden, Labour MP for Blackburn, whose wife Ethel, formerly Ethel Annakin, was an active suffragette, was also in favour. He pointed out that this was the twenty-third occasion that the question of female enfranchisement had been debated since John Stuart Mill moved his Amendment to the Reform Bill of 1867. On each of these twenty-three occasions the same worm-eaten objections had been brought forward. In the intervening years those objections had been disproved by the hard logic of facts. To Mallet's list of countries that had already given the vote to women, Snowden added one he had forgotten to mention, Norway. Snowden drew a different conclusion to that of Mallet; in none of these countries had the anticipations and fears which had so often been expressed been realised: 'The stockings still got darned, the baby was still nursed.'

Fred Pethick Lawrence noted the change in atmosphere in the House of Commons; the right of women to vote was being seriously discussed for the very first time:

> The debate ... marked a new phase of the question; not because of the result arrived at, but because of the change of the attitude of the House of Commons. I attended the debate in 1907, and I was present on this occasion, and heard the whole of the speeches. The change between the two discussions was most remarkable. This year the question was treated by every member, with one exception, as a serious question of practical politics, in favour of which and against which arguments had to be brought forward.
>
> But still more important than this change from the levity of previous years was the sense of the growing importance of the women's agitation which pervaded the atmosphere of the Chamber, and was detected even in the speeches of the most vigorous opponents of the Bill. Scarcely a single speech was made in which some reference to the militant agitation was not made and the general feeling among the members was that however much they might disapprove of the action of the Suffragettes, nevertheless the leaders were women whose characters were above suspicion, and whose outlook was political, and not due to any desire for personal advantage.

Emmeline Pankhurst thought that the MPs had advanced several reasons against giving women the vote, all of which she naturally refuted. The most fundamental was the oldest: that the security of Government rests ultimately on force, which women could not provide. One response would have been to demand the introduction of women into the armed forces, but this would have seemed unthinkable a century ago. Mrs Pankhurst took a different line:

> With the progress of civilisation spiritual force replaces physical force as the controlling element in human affairs, and at the present day physical force is brought into play only for the purpose of restraining those anti-social and less highly evolved members of the community who are not amenable to any more subtle form of control. To this order of being, Members of Parliament who argue that Government rests on force unwittingly confess themselves to belong.

The spring of 1908 saw a new Prime Minister: Campbell-Bannerman had resigned because of ill health and was replaced by Herbert Asquith. This was bad news for the campaigners as Asquith was known for his opposition to women's suffrage; however, it did mean several by-elections. In those days, a new Cabinet minister resigned his seat and submitted to a by-election before entering office. New Cabinet members named by Asquith included Winston Churchill, which meant a by-election in his constituency of North West Manchester. The suffragettes, led by Christabel Pankhurst, took an active part in the campaign and Churchill was indeed defeated: the Government had to find him a safe seat in Dundee from which to continue his political career.

The summer of 1908 brought great protest marches in London. On 13 June, the NUWSS sponsored a procession in London in which 10,000 women took part. This was overshadowed by the meeting held in Hyde Park on 21 June by the WSPU. Every avenue of propaganda was exploited. The WSPU now introduced its own colours, purple, white and green, conceived by Emmeline Pethick-Lawrence, 'which, selected in the middle of May, had achieved a nation-wide familiarity before the month was out'. The other groups soon followed, the WFL adopting yellow, white and green, the NUWSS red, white and green. As we have seen, the suffrage newspapers were soon carrying advertisements for coats and even for underwear in the appropriate colours!

People from all over the country were brought to London by thirty special trains, and formed into seven processions converging on the park. Flora Drummond had been placed in charge of organising processions for 'Women's Sunday'; her flair and enthusiasm earned her the nickname 'General', which she proudly adopted. From this point, she was rarely given any other name, and completed her military persona by regularly sporting a peaked cap, epaulettes, and a sash embroidered 'general', all in the WSPU colours. A skilled horsewoman, she often rode at the head of WSPU processions in her regalia, or reviewed her suffragette 'troops' on horseback. It was an undoubted triumph for the cause; Fred Pethick-Lawrence noted that 'it was admitted on all sides that the numbers who came to the park that day were greater than had ever been gathered together before on any one spot in the whole history of the world'.

The marches were reported on at length in *The Times*:

The National Union of Women's Suffrage Societies showed the capacity of women to organise a beautiful and impressive procession through the streets of London, and yesterday the more militant National Women's Social and Political Union made an even more imposing appeal to the attention of the public by their remarkable demonstration in Hyde Park. Seven processions from various points in London converged on the Park and, although their appearance was but sorry compared to the march from the Embankment to the Albert-hall, this was amply counterbalanced by their numbers, reckoned at about 30,000. In the Park itself the testimony of observers, including our own Correspondent, agrees that no such crowd has been seen in any previous meeting there within the last quarter of a century. For here, in addition to the 30,000 demonstrators, thousands of men and women, some sympathetic, some merely curious, and some openly hostile, had gathered to swell the numbers. A quarter of a million, indeed, seems to be hardly an exaggerated figure at which to place this immense crowd gathered round the twenty platforms from which well-known advocates of the cause addressed those near enough to hear them. Again we can but offer a tribute of admiration to the wonderful skill in organisation displayed by those responsible for this remarkable demonstration, especially to their chief, Mrs Drummond, and at the same time to the management by the police of this enormous crowd. Certainly Mr Asquith's advice is bearing fruit. It would be idle to deny, after the object-lessons of June 13 and yesterday, that a great many women are for the time being eagerly desirous of the franchise, though, of course, 30,000 demonstrators and a crowd of a quarter of a million to watch them is no proof such as the Prime Minister required, to the effect that an overwhelming majority of the women of this country demanded the vote.

Political opinion, however, is apt to be unduly swayed by large crowds, especially in the metropolis, and it is certainly time that a corresponding demonstration of strength, not necessarily by the same methods, should be made by the women who disbelieve in the suitability of their sex for the franchise, and by the men of the same opinion, whose views have also to be considered.

However, the paper was still against giving the vote to women:

We cannot recede from our opinion that women are less strong in persistence and in physical power than men owing to the great demands made upon them by nature for their greatest constitutional function and their greatest service to the State. We believe that it would weaken the moral fibre of the nation if the supreme decisions of the State were determined partly by women who could not feel the same responsibility for seeing them carried through as men, and partly by men who would insensibly lose the feeling of direct responsibility which most citizens have and which cannot be too much encouraged, when once they realized that their determinations were to some extent neutralized by those who were less responsible.

Sylvia Pankhurst described the occasion in her usual fervent prose:

Every circumstance conspired to make the occasion attractive. The weather was beautifully fine; and the park was in the height of its summer glory; but if there had not been in addition a powerful human interest to make appeal to the public, such a spectacle as that of yesterday would be impossible. Anyone who witnessed it must have felt amply repaid for any exertion made in getting to the park and any weariness endured in standing about for two or three hours on end in a dense and surging mass of humanity. If the demonstration proved nothing else, it would prove incontestably that the suffragists have acquired great skill in the art of popular agitation ... There may be various views as to what this demonstration has proved; but there can be no differences as to its magnitude, its organization, and its success. The women of London were exhorted to go to Hyde Park with the assurance that the memory of the occasion would be one to hand down to their children and their grand-children. No one who responded to the invitation will deny that that assurance at least was amply fulfilled.

The behaviour of the people was, on the whole, remarkably orderly and good-humoured. There was indeed one person who went about ringing a muffin-bell; but his scope for mischief was not large. There was, too, a considerable dissentient element, but its interruptions were so promptly and effectively taken up that it was baffled of its purpose. More serious was the exuberance of certain groups of youth, of the type familiar in every London crowd, who imagine that their cleverness is shown by 'guying' whatever is going on. Individually contemptible, they are formidable in a mass; and yesterday they made themselves felt by chanting in unison some refrain while the speeches were going on, and by joining, in the intervals, in rushes and horse-play. But the crowds gathered round the platforms were too dense to permit them to effect much mischief.

Window-Breaking Begins

After the June demonstration, Emmeline Pankhurst realised that the WSPU had 'exhausted argument'; the next step in the campaign was about to be taken. Another Women's Parliament took place on 30 June and then, at 4.30 p.m., Mrs Pankhurst led another deputation to Asquith which was repulsed from the Commons. That evening, in Parliament Square, women were roughly handled by the police as they made speeches, some twenty-five being arrested. Outraged by the police brutality, Mary Leigh and Edith New each threw a stone through a window at Asquith's official residence at 10 Downing Street; they were arrested and sentenced to two months in prison. The two women sent word to Emmeline Pankhurst that, having acted without orders, they would not resent her repudiation of their acts. Far from repudiating them, Emmeline went at once to see them in their cells and 'assured them' of her approval. She wrote, 'The smashing of windows is a time-honoured method of showing displeasure in a political situation ... Window-breaking, when Englishmen do it, is regarded as an honest expression of opinion. Window-breaking, when Englishwomen do it, is treated as a crime.' However, this weapon was not to become WSPU policy on a large scale until 1913.

The WSPU now adopted a programme of increasing 'violence'; this violence was always aimed against property, *never* against people. Every act of arson by the WSPU was carefully planned by the organisation, who were determined that 'not a cat, dog or canary' would be harmed. This was faithfully carried out; the only people ever harmed were the suffragettes themselves. By no means all members of the WSPU were in favour of even this amount of aggression, and several members resigned in protest. The NUWSS made a definite break with the WSPU after the suffragettes abandoned their policy of suffering violence but using none. The Women's Freedom League fell between the two, preferring publicity-attracting 'stunts' to actual damage to property.

The Rush on Parliament

In October 1908, the WSPU issued a handbill inviting people to 'help the suffragettes rush the House of Commons' on the evening of 13 October. A crowd of about 60,000 turned up and were met by some 5,000 police; groups of suffragettes tried to make their way into the House of Commons. Clara Codd, a suffragette from Bristol, actually managed to enter the House before she was arrested.

About thirty-six people – men and women – were arrested, including Emmeline and Christabel Pankhurst and Flora Drummond. On 14 October, they were tried at Bow Street, charged with 'inciting to disorder' based upon the handbill that had been published. The case was postponed until 21 October; the three accused did not employ counsel but conducted their own defence. As she rose to speak, Emmeline assumed an appearance of calm that she did not feel. Then she made a poignant speech, relating her life experiences as a working mother and as a Poor Law Guardian, where she had learnt about the unjust marriage and divorce laws that deprived women of maintenance for their children and gave them no legal right of guardianship. She stressed how she and other WSPU members had tried to be patient and 'womanly', using constitutional methods, all to no avail, and pleaded, 'We have taken this action, because as women … we realise that the condition of our sex is so deplorable that it is our duty to break the law in order to call attention to the reasons why we do so. We are here not because we are law-breakers; we are here in our efforts to become law-makers.'

At the trial, Christabel called as witnesses some of the greatest names in England – the Home Secretary, Herbert Gladstone, and the Chancellor of the Exchequer, David Lloyd George. The cross-examinations attracted enormous interest and were fully reported in the press – a 'suffrage meeting attended by millions', commented Emmeline Pethick-Lawrence. Although Christabel's brilliant advocacy earned her the nickname of 'Portia in the dock', it was her mother's pleading that moved her listeners to tears. No mercy was shown, however, and all three defendants were sent to prison. They were released in December, which was the occasion for a triumphal procession round the West End.

Millicent Fawcett was shocked by the turn of events, writing in a private letter to a friend,

On the reassembling of Parliament, the well-known attempt to 'rush the House of Commons' was made and in anticipation of this handbills were distributed among the lowest classes of London toughs and dangerous hordes of unemployed containing the invitation to 'rush the House of Commons'. I have never said in public and to very few people in private what I thought of that proceeding; but I tell you in confidence that I considered it is [*sic*] immoral and dastardly thing to have done. The House of Commons, with all its faults, stands for order against anarchy, for justice against brutality, and to overcome it and to invite others to endeavour to overcome it by brute force of the lowest ruffians in London was in my opinion the act either of a mad woman or of a dastard. It became evident to me that our organization must separate itself entirely from all cooperation with people who would resort to such weapons … It is not by such weapons as these that we stand to win. They have helped the antis and discouraged their friends. The crimes committed in Ireland by Home Rulers stopped Home Rule and if Women Suffragists embark on crime as propaganda, they will stop Women's Suffrage.

In November the NUWSS publicly disavowed the methods of the militants.

Meanwhile, the Women's Freedom League were active. On 27 October, they tried to hold a meeting in Old Palace Yard in Westminster. Jenny McCallum was one of four WFL members arrested; they were fined, refused to pay, and were sentenced to a month in prison. On the following day, the WFL pulled off one of its most spectacular stunts. Even Sylvia Pankhurst was approving:

On October 28th Muriel Matters and Helen Fox, both of the Women's Freedom League, were in the Ladies' Gallery of the House of Commons. They managed to thrust a large poster proclaiming Woman's Rights through the iron grille separating the gallery from the debating chamber, and Muriel startled the House of Commons by delivering a speech from the Ladies' Gallery. An attendant rushed to eject her, but found they had chained themselves to the historic grille by which the occupants of the Ladies' Gallery were discreetly hidden from the Members.

As Sylvia put it, 'The padlock was a Yale, the chain was strong.'

An attendant gagged the disturber with his hands, while his colleagues made ineffectual efforts to dislodge her. Another woman began to speak; she too had chained herself. It was necessary to clear the gallery and dismember the grille. The offenders were brought out with the heavy pieces of wrought brass to which they were fastened, and kept in a committee room till a smith was procured to file through their chains. Meanwhile Violet Tillard showered the floor of the Commons with leaflets advocating women's suffrage while other WFL members protested outside the House. Women attempted to hold a meeting in the lobby and, when thrown out, climbed up to speak on the pedestal of the statue of King Richard the Lionheart. While the police were clambering after some of them, others rushed into the House. As a result of these episodes, fourteen women received a month's imprisonment, and the Speaker ordered that the public galleries, both for men and women, should be closed.

This was an excellent propaganda event by the WFL because of the significance of the grille. There were separate galleries for men and women spectators in the House of Commons – but only the women's gallery had a grille fitted! A supporter, Laurence Houseman, wrote in *Votes For Women*, 'there was the barrier which had for so long been set up for a protection actually providing the means by which the intruders were able to make their protest known to all the world'.

Another form of activity especially associated with the WFL was the caravan tour, where a number of suffragists would use a horse-drawn vehicle to go to the smaller towns and villages and promote the cause; in the days when people had no radio, let alone television or the internet, such means were the only way to reach into the rural heartlands. The WFL had a specially built caravan, drawn by a horse named Asquith! Those inhabiting it at various times included Lilian Hicks, Muriel Matters, Alison Neilans, Marguerite Sidley and even Mrs Despard herself. They did not have a monopoly on this form of propaganda. The NUWSS also had caravans, including one described as 'very elegant and comfortable with its three berths, one of which was also a linen chest; its art nouveau curtains and its green canvas walls'. The WSPU seem to have been less enthusiastic caravanners, although Elsie Howey did present a caravan to their Midlands branch in 1909.

Not every woman was a suffragette. Indeed, as Bertrand Russell had pointed out, although no slaves appear to have campaigned against the abolition of slavery, there were women prepared to campaign *against* being given the vote.

The Women's National Anti-Suffrage League was launched in July 1908, becoming the National League for Opposing Woman Suffrage (open to both men and women) from 1910. Its leader was Mary Ward, and it had its own journal, the *Anti-Suffrage Review*, launched in December 1908. By 1910, the group had over 100 branches and between 15,000 and 20,000 members. In June 1914, after six years' work, the league claimed to have 42,000 subscribing members and 15,000 adherents.

The women held debates and organised petitions and canvasses to try and show that the majority of women did not want the vote. A petition begun in 1908 had received 430,808 votes (men and women) by 1913, not all of genuine supporters; one woman in Hampstead wrote to *The Times* complaining that 'my servants, in my absence, were invited to sign the anti-suffrage petition, the nature of which was not disclosed to them'. Suffrage supporters conducted their own canvasses – which always had the opposite outcomes.

Another member was Ethel Harrison, who wrote to a supporter, Lord Curzon, after a male supporter had resigned from the cause: 'Our society must in the main depend upon women. Women have to destroy a women's movement.' In 1908 she wrote 'The Freedom of Women', one of the key texts of the anti-suffrage movement.

The Women's National Anti-Suffrage League put forward seven arguments *against* giving women the vote:

1. The spheres of men and women are essentially different.
2. Women could not take any practical part in running a

'complex modern State' which relied on naval and military power, diplomacy, finance, and the great mining, constructive, shipping and transport industries.

3. Women had already been given enough opportunity to be politically active, through the municipal vote and their admission to local councils.

4. The influence of women 'in social causes will be diminished rather than increased by the possession of the parliamentary vote'.

5. To enfranchise women on the same terms as men would 'in practice involve an unjust and invidious limitation'; but enfranchising voters' wives would only introduce political disagreement into the home; while adult suffrage would mean that women voters would outnumber the men!

6. Women's suffrage was a dangerous experiment, not worth the risk.

7. Women did not need the vote to cure their wrongs – 'all the reforms which are put forward as reasons for the vote can be obtained by other means than the vote, as is proved by the general history of the laws relating to women and children during the past century'.

While some women were opposing the suffrage movement, some men were actively supporting it. They took part in meetings, supported protest marches and supplied funds; they could join the NUWSS, but the WSPU did not take men as members. Many other groups also took both men and women, such as groups based on political parties or church affiliations. Other groups were specifically for men, such as the Men's League for Women's Suffrage and the Men's Political Union. Edward Hicks, the Bishop of Lincoln, was an active campaigner for women's suffrage, as his diary records: '1912, July 16: I took chair at meeting of the Church League for Women's Suffrage: Miss Royden spoke *beautifully*.' He preached on the subject at Oxford on 3 November 1912, noting that it was 'boomed' by the press, eight provincial and London journals ordering reports. He was in London on 23 January 1913 and 'saw the women's Deputation leaving their interview with Lloyd George & other ministers: many women "picketing" the House of C. Scores of *Ladies* with sandwich boards, with mottoes e.g. "Labour men we confide in your courtesy, and we thank you", etc.'

A few men were prepared to go further, taking part in window-smashing activities and arson, going to prison, and even, in a small number of cases, going on hunger strike. There are forty men out of 1,097 names on a list drawn up of suffragette prisoners between 1905 and 1914. Not all women welcomed the support of men; Christabel Pankhurst, for one, saw men primarily as protagonists to be fought against. Once she was being heckled in Hyde Park by a man who then threw a cabbage at her. Holding it up, she said calmly, 'I knew *that* man would lose his head!'

Neither the women who campaigned against the vote nor the men who campaigned for women to have the vote receive much attention today, but neither group should be forgotten.

5

1909: The Weapon of Self-Harm

On 17 February 1909, Muriel Matters pulled off a second spectacular stunt. She hired an airship, with a pilot, which had the words 'VOTES FOR WOMEN' painted on its side and flew from Hendon over Central London and over Parliament dropping suffrage leaflets; as it was the first day of the new session in Parliament, this was a particularly dramatic gesture.

Both the WFL and WSPU presented yet more petitions to Parliament, with supporters facing arrest as they made their point. Those arrested on 24 February included Charlotte Despard, Emmeline Pethick-Lawrence and Lady Constance Lytton. Many people thought that suffragette leaders like these received preferential treatment in comparison with rank-and-file members. This was so in Lady Lytton's case; she spent her time in prison in the Hospital Ward because she had a heart condition. Eventually, she insisted on being put in a prison cell like the other suffragettes.

As always, a release from Holloway became a celebration. On 16 April, suffragettes and their supporters gathered to celebrate the release of Mrs Pethick-Lawrence. Sylvia Pankhurst wrote,

What a day it was to welcome anyone from prison. The trees were just bursting into leaf, and the brilliant April sunshine glistened on the silver armour of Elsie Howey, who represented Joan of Arc, the warrior maid, whose beatification was taking place that very day, and rode at the head of the procession, astride her great white charger, with the brisk wind blowing back her fair hair, and gaily fluttering the purple-white-and-green standard that she bore.

The ideal suffragette stunt at this stage was one which attracted a lot of publicity but involved no violence. A good example occurred at this time; two suffragettes posted themselves from the Strand to Downing Street under a new Post Office regulation allowing the posting and delivery of human letters! On 23 January, Jessie Kenney (Annie's sister) went to the Post Office, applied to send a human letter and posted her companions, Georgiana Solomon and Miss McLellan, to Asquith at 10 Downing Street, SW. 'The threepenny fee having been paid, a telegraph messenger was summoned and the women delivered into his charge, with the injunction that the signature of the consignee must be obtained on delivery,' *Votes for Women* reported. The telegraph boy marched into the Strand towards Whitehall, a suffragette on either side of him. One woman bore a poster card announcing Wednesday evening's demonstration, while the other had a 'destination card' with the Prime Minister's name and address in bold black letters. Upon their arrival at Downing Street, Asquith's butler told the women, 'You must be returned.' The women protested, 'But we have been paid for.' 'Well, then,' the butler replied, 'the Post Office must deliver you somewhere else. You can't be delivered here.' The women continued to protest, but the butler insisted, 'You must be returned. You are dead letters.' The women then returned to the WSPU offices at Clement's Inn.

As the years passed, new local suffrage societies were continually being founded, such as that in Great Yarmouth. The first meeting was held in May 1909 and members included a number of redoubtable seaside landladies as well as teachers and the wives of clergymen. They listened to talks by people like Muriel Matters and other suffragette leaders, passed resolutions condemning the Government's treatment of prisoners, and held public meetings. The chairman was Ethel Leach, a good example of what a determined woman could accomplish at a local level. A friend of Helen Taylor, she had been her campaign manager in the 1885 Parliamentary election. In 1881, Ethel became the first woman on Yarmouth School Board and was also one of the first women to serve on the Yarmouth Board of Guardians. In later life, she became the borough's first female mayor. It may be argued that the efficient service to the community by such women contributed at least as much to the eventual success of the cause as the spectacular stunts of militant campaigners. A group like that at Yarmouth also illustrates an important fact; outside London, the societies were not the bitter rivals that they sometimes appear. They would co-operate at a local level to promote the cause, and a group like that at Yarmouth would invite speakers from any of the main societies.

On 19 March there was a new attempt in Parliament to obtain the suffrage; this was the second reading of Geoffrey Howard's Electoral Reform Bill proposing votes for women. Despite a vote in favour, Asquith made it clear that such a Bill would only be acceptable as a Government measure. This led to an increase in one form of suffragette activity: the disruption and heckling of meetings by Cabinet ministers. This might impress upon them how much women cared about the cause, or they might give in, it was hoped, if only for the sake of peace and quiet. It could have the opposite effect, however: Winston Churchill is supposed to have grown to dislike the campaign for women's suffrage because women were continually interrupting his carefully prepared and high-flown speeches!

Summer is the time for marching; there was another great parade in Hyde Park and march to the Albert Hall on Saturday 18 June. Sylvia Pankhurst recalled,

We flocked to Hyde Park. The ground was already thronged with an unprecedented mass of human beings; we had difficulty in making our way to the platform with our banners. As far as the eye could reach was a mass of human beings ... the predominating gay hues of the women's clothes and the white straw hats of the men suggested a giant bed of flowers. Under that golden sunshine, that sky of cloudless blue, it was a gala day indeed. From a furniture van – Pethick Lawrence had called it a conning-tower, but it looked a tiny speck in the mass – bugles sounded for the commencement and ending of the speeches. Then came the great shout: 'VOTES FOR WOMEN!' three times repeated. All went with a swing. Only a few young rowdies at the platforms of Christabel and Mrs Pankhurst attempted ineffectually to mar the great good humour of the day.

We were buoyed by delighted triumph in this success, and belief of an early victory for the cause. Self was forgotten; personality seemed minute, the movement so big, so splendid. What an achievement! This without doubt was the greatest meeting ever known.

The press described the occasion in enthusiastic terms:

The Times: 'Its organisers had counted on an audience of 250,000. That expectation was certainly fulfilled; probably it was doubled; it would be difficult to contradict anyone who asserted that it was trebled. Like the distance and number of the stars, the facts were beyond the threshold of perception.'

Daily News: 'There is no combination of words which will convey an adequate immensity of the crowd around the platforms.'

Daily Express: 'The Women Suffragists provided London yesterday with one of the most wonderful and astonishing sights that has ever been seen since the days of Boadicea … It is probable that so many people never before stood in one square mass anywhere in England.'

Such events attracted younger people into the movement. Esther Knowles, aged thirteen, was present at the Albert Hall:

Wearing a white dress, and the widest purple white and green as I could get I had marched in the children's contingent of the procession, in spite of my father's disapproval. I had sold

Votes for Women outside the Hall before the meeting, then
I had helped to steward people to their seats in the balcony,
and now I stood gazing down into the vast auditorium. The
leaders on the platforms looked like pygmies and the heads
of the audience swayed like a field of summer grasses below
me.

When Esther returned home late that evening, she found her
parents had had an argument about her attendance at the
event, which her father had 'resolved' by physical violence,
hitting her mother. Despite this parental opposition, Esther
soon became the youngest worker at the WSPU office. Alice
Kedge, a fourteen-year-old servant from Camden Town,
bought a 'Votes for Women' badge – when her mother told
her to throw it away, she wore it under her coat as she did
not want to upset her mother, and could not afford to lose
her job.

The march was followed on 29 June by what has become
known as the 'Bill of Rights' deputation. Mrs Pankhurst
and eight well-known women attempted to take a petition
to Parliament, claiming that 'it is the right of the subject
to petition the king'; the deputation was rejected. In the
evening, groups of suffragettes gathered; according to the
author Antonia Raeburn, 'each woman was issued with a
striped denim Dorothy bag containing stones wrapped in
brown paper and tied with string. The Dorothy bags were
attached round the waist under the skirt and at the signal
for the 'smash up', the stones could be reached through a
placket pocket.' Ada Wright, one of the stone-throwers,
recalled,

To women of culture and of sheltered upbringing the deliberate throwing of a stone, even as a protest, in order to break a window, requires an enormous amount of moral courage. After much tension and hesitation, I threw my stone through the window of the Office of Works. To my relief I was at once arrested and marched off by two policemen, the tremendous crowd making way for us and cheering to the echo, all the way to Cannon Row Police Station.

Another stone-thrower was Sarah Carwin, who broke windows in a Government building – and on being taken to Holloway broke every pane in her cell window. Emmeline Pankhurst wrote to her, 'Women have reason to be grateful that you and others have the courage to play the soldier's part in the war we are waging for the political freedom of women.'

Altogether, 108 arrests were made. In the police court, the women claimed their action was justified by the Bill of Rights. All but the stone-throwers were bailed, and the case referred to the High Court. The test case of Emmeline Pankhurst and Evelina Haverfield was heard in December, Evelina's lawyer claiming that she had been wrongfully arrested in the exercise of a constitutional right. However, the leaders were found guilty and fined, the cases of the other women being dismissed. In the words of Mrs Pankhurst, 'Thus was destroyed in England the ancient constitutional right of petition, secured to the people by the Bill of Rights, and cherished by uncounted generations of Englishmen. I say the right was destroyed, for of how much value is a petition which cannot be presented in person?'

In July 1909 there came a new step in the struggle, the one for which it is probably best remembered today: the hunger strike. Annie Kenney was clear that the hunger strike was a vital new weapon in the suffragette campaign:

Nineteen hundred and nine will always be remembered by me [Kenney]. It was in this year that Miss Wallace Dunlop, an artist, conceived the idea of the hunger strike. This weapon, which was to play a great part in our policy, was not thought of by Christabel, but by one of her most ardent admirers. Miss Wallace Dunlop went to prison, and defied the long sentences that were being given by adopting the hunger-strike. 'Release or Death' was her motto. When asked by the prison authorities what she would have for dinner, her reply was, 'My own determination.' From that day, July 5th 1909, the hunger-strike was the greatest weapon we possessed against the Government ... before long all Suffragette prisoners were on hunger-strike, so the threat to pass long sentences on us had failed.

Marion Wallace Dunlop was imprisoned for rubber-stamping a passage from the Bill of Rights onto the wall at St Stephen's Hall. She went on hunger strike to protest at the Government's failure to grant her political prisoner status. She recalled the first day:

I threw a fried fish, four slices of bread, three bananas and a cup of hot milk out of my window on Tuesday, that being the only day I really felt hungry. They threatened all the time to pump milk through my nostrils, but never did. They kept my table covered with food, which I never touched. I only drank water. My pulse was felt many times in the day and I laughed at them all the time, telling them I would show them the stuff the Suffragette was made of; and that they would either have to put me in the first division or release me.

She was released after 91 hours.

Votes for Women noted that Dunlop was a 'direct descendant of the mother of William Wallace', the Scottish resistance fighter (best known today as 'Braveheart', thanks to the Mel Gibson film). It said that, 'being refused recognition of her status as a political prisoner, she decided to adopt the drastic expedient of the hunger strike ... by that splendid action she has made it easier for all the political prisoners who come after her'.

Marion was soon followed by others, including a number of the women in prison for throwing stones through glass windows. One of the stone-throwers, Gladys Roberts, from Leeds, kept a diary:

12 July: On arriving at Holloway, we were taken into the corridor outside the reception cells. Our names were called and we answered. Miss Wright then asked to see the governor. The wardress, who had tow-coloured hair and was very disagreeable, fetched the matron who wanted us to answer to our names again. We refused and asked once more to see the governor. At last he was sent for. On hearing from Miss Wright that we intended to rebel against all the second-division rules, the governor said he would let us keep

our clothing and bags until he communicated with the Home Secretary if we went quietly to our cells ...

13 July: Breakfast just arrived which consists of another lump of that horrible brown bread and tea. I read *Votes* and tried to eat some of the bread, but failed ... Tea consisted of the usual loaf. I could only manage a few crumbs – it's so vile – my fat will soon be reduced!

On 13/14 July, the stone-throwers in Holloway went on hunger strike. Their actions had been pre-arranged. Gladys Roberts stood on a chair, like the others in their own cells, and smashed the glass windowpanes with her shoe. The next day (14 July), she wrote,

A magistrate has been to see Miss Spong – one of those who were about to try us for mutiny. He told her that he knew we were right, but that he would have to punish us. My bag and hat were taken from me by six wardresses. I told the magistrates I was not sorry for breaking windows, and that I did not intend to comply with any second-division rules, so was sentenced to seven days' close confinement and was brought down to this cell, with nothing in it except a block of wood fixed to the wall for a chair and a plank bed and pillow ... unbreakable opaque windows and double iron doors – God help me to stick it! I can hear the others singing, thank goodness!

Her diary continues,

They have brought us a pint of cocoa and a lump of the usual bread. Hunger strike commences. The drum and fife band is coming at eight o'clock. I wonder if I shall hear it. We seem to be buried alive.

15 July: I lie on the bed – I feel so weak – breakfast has just been put in. I said I didn't want any. God help me! I wonder if those outside are thinking of us ... I hear knocking on the walls, and all the prisoners are shouting that they have not eaten their food. Neither have I. Dinner consisted of an egg and potatoes and a pint of milk and (oh, awful temptation!) a boiled onion. I am getting disinclined to write even.

16 July: The wardress said to me this morning, 'Get your clothes on. We shall want to take your bed out.' I wonder if they will. Miss Carwin didn't have hers all day yesterday. Part of the process seems to be to degrade us by not allowing us to wash properly. This morning I have had only my drinking can of water to wash in ... I saw through the peephole, which was accidentally left open, Mrs Holtwhite Simmons go out of the cell opposite looking ghastly. I wonder if I look likewise. Fifty-four hours without food! God help me to hold out!

17 July: I can't get up this morning. The cleaner came and swept out my cell. She smiled at me and it made me so weepy. The doctor has been and tried to persuade me to give up the hunger strike by saying that I was not so robust as the others. What would my mother and father say and so on ... It is now seventy-two hours since I tasted food. The governor and matron have just been to say that Herbert Gladstone had written that he has fully considered the petitions, but sees no reason why he should take action in the matter which proves he could, if he would. Tremendous excitement – Mary Allen has just come down to the cell next to mine. She broke more

windows when she heard Herbert Gladstone's reply. It has quite bucked me up.

18 July: Had a fairly good night, but dreaming of food all the time. I feel more cheerful today. I've had quite long talks with Mary Allen through the wall. We've beaten Miss Wallace Dunlop's record! Dinner time today will be ninety-six hours without food ...

19 July: I had rather a bad night. The bed, I was sure, must be stuffed with stones, and my poor bones ached terribly. At a little after twelve o'clock, just after dinner had been thrust in, the hospital matron and two prisoners with a carrying chair came for me and carried me to the hospital. They put me to bed and gave me a hot water bottle and brought me jelly, milk, and bread and butter, which of course I refused.

At 6.20 p.m. that evening, the governor said to her, 'Are you still obstinate?' and when she answered, 'Yes,' told that he had good news; she was about to be released. An hour later she was set free and taken in a cab to some friends in Clement's Inn. The majority of the other hunger strikers were released within a week.

The impression is sometimes given that the key events in the campaign took place in London, but there were outbreaks of 'violence' of various kinds against Cabinet ministers all over the country. We can consider just a few of those occurring in the second half of 1909, beginning with a hunger strike in Exeter Prison in July. Three 'young militant suffragettes' were arrested for disturbing a public meeting with Earl Carrington, a Government minister, at Victoria Hall in Exeter; anticipating trouble, he had banned women from the meeting. They were Mary Phillips, Elsie Howey and Vera Wentworth. The police arrested the three women who disobeyed, and two men who tried to help them. They had attempted to storm the doors to get in and were charged with obstruction. The women were found guilty and taken to Exeter Prison; there they went on hunger strike, refusing food unless they were given political prisoner status. They also refused to go to their cells or to put on prison dress. The prison staff threatened to force-feed them through the nose, but the women were defiant. They sang songs, caused destruction in the prison and after several days were allowed to leave because of their weak conditions. Exeter historian and author Dr Todd Gray noted that 'the hunger strike has been overlooked by historians and is not remembered today but it was hugely influential in Exeter at the time ... It was part of the long local campaign by women for the right to vote ... The suffragettes were women who were celebrated for their beauty, but behind that they had keen, sharp minds and were able to turn anything to their advantage.'

In September 1909, Elsie Howey and two other women climbed into Lympne Castle, Kent, where Asquith was staying, and demanded 'votes for women' through the dining-room window while the family was at dinner; they then escaped via an adjacent canal.

Asquith was involved in a much less frivolous episode at Birmingham in the same month, and one which saw the Government make its response to the weapon of the hunger strike. On 17 September, barricades were erected in Birmingham in anticipation of disturbances during Asquith's visit. Charlotte Marsh and Mary Leigh showered down slates from nearby roofs onto the roof of Bingley Hall, where the Prime Minister was to speak. *The Times* reported,

> Two young women at great personal risk got onto the roof of a factory in Cambridge Street, opposite the hall, and began throwing stones at the police below. A fire escape [ladder] was sent for as they refused to come down, and a jet of water was turned on to them. They, however, refused to come down, but hid themselves behind a chimney. Several police officers followed them on to the roof, and they were brought down and taken to Ladywood police station … Their clothing was very wet, and after they had received the attention of the female searcher they were placed in a cell. Here they again became very violent and smashed a number of windows.

Meanwhile three other women – Laura Ainsworth, a local schoolteacher, Evelyn Wurrie and Patricia Woodlock – were arrested for smashing windows at the Liberal Club in Lower Temple Street. Five other women were also arrested – Mary Edwards, Leslie Hall, Mabel Capper, Ellen Barnwell and Hilda Burkitt. The latter two had gone to the train station and hurled missiles at the train bearing Asquith as he left Birmingham; they had shattered the glass, but it was not the compartment in which the Prime Minister was travelling. The women were all sentenced to one month's imprisonment in the second division.

The women were sent to Winson Green Prison, where they went on hunger strike. On 24 September, prison authorities began forcibly feeding them. This was a new development. The first was Mary Leigh; this was her third hunger strike but the first time the authorities had responded not by setting her free but by force-feeding. She described the experience to her solicitor:

> On Saturday afternoon the wardresses forced me on to the bed and the two doctors came in with them. While I was held down a nasal tube was inserted. It is two yards long with a funnel at the end; there is a glass junction in the middle to see if the liquid is passing. The end is put up the right and left nostril on alternate days. Great pain is experienced during the process, both mental and physical. One doctor inserted the end up my nostril while I was held down by the wardresses, during which process they must have seen my pain, for the other doctor interfered (the matron and two of the wardresses were in tears), and they stopped and resorted to feeding me by spoon, as in the morning ... On Sunday [the doctor] came in and implored me to be amenable and have food in the proper way. I still refused.

Another hunger striker to be forcibly fed was Laura Ainsworth, who made her experience public upon her release:

> There were two doctors and six wardresses in addition to the matron. The prison doctor said, 'I have orders that you are not to be released. I have to do everything in my power to feed you. I am going to commit a technical assault, and I take full responsibility for my action.' He then asked, 'Will you take food or not?' 'No,' I said emphatically. Whereupon, I was sounded, and my pulse taken. Afterwards, I was placed

in a chair, my head was held back by the wardresses, and one of the doctors opened my mouth by inserting his finger between the teeth at one side. Milk was poured down my throat by means of a feeding cup. While this was being done, both my mouth and nose were held. I was then put to bed. Afterwards, the governor asked me if I had any complaints to make, and when I complained of this treatment, he simply referred me to the visiting justices.

At six o'clock on the Saturday evening, the two doctors returned. I again refused to take food out of the cup, and resisted their efforts to make me take it. Then they tried to force tubes into my nostrils. There seemed to be something sharp at the end of these tubes, and I felt a sharp, pricking sensation. Owing to an injury received before going into gaol through someone hitting me on the nose with a stone, it appeared the nasal passage was closed. One of the doctors said; 'It's no good. We shall have to use the tube.'

I was raised into a sitting position, and the tube about two feet long was produced. My mouth was prized open with what felt like a steel instrument, and then I felt them feeling for the proper passage. All this time, I was held down by four or five wardresses. I felt a choking sensation, and what I judged to be a cork gag was placed between my teeth to keep my mouth open. It was a horrible feeling altogether. I experienced great sickness, especially when the tube was being withdrawn.

Force-feeding has attracted much philosophical and psychological commentary. The hunger strikers have been described as 'performance artists', using their whole bodies in their cause, and comparisons have been made with the force-feeding we all undergo as babies. It can best be seen as an inhuman and degrading torture performed by a male doctor on an unwilling woman. Naturally, many people compared it with rape; a few women, such as Fanny Parker in Perth Prison, were even forcibly fed through tubes pushed into the vagina or the rectum. Many women suffered from injuries caused by the insertion of the tubes, some never fully recovering. Maud Kate Smith was force-fed in Winson Green – a tube forced up her nostrils damaged the membrane of her nose which still bled sixty years later. Afterwards they put the tube down her throat – she suffered such intense pain that she was thrown across the cell! She was then held down by wardresses so she could not move a muscle. She recalled that one woman became paralysed in her legs after being forcibly fed. Some women never fully recovered: Mary Blathwayt's family house at Batheaston in Somerset was opened up to hunger strikers, who could recuperate there after their ordeal. Many of them planted trees there, each with a plaque recording the occasion; sadly this grove of trees no longer survives.

The process made the Government hateful in the minds of many; two leading journalists, H. N. Brailsford and H. W. Nevinson, resigned from the *Daily News* in protest. However, the only alternative for the Government would have been to let the prisoners starve to death, which, in its view, would only have created so many martyrs for the cause. It took four years for the authorities to come up with a different policy to counter the weapon of the hunger strike.

There were many other cases of disturbances involving Cabinet ministers. On 4 October, women graduates in Manchester protested when Lord Morley visited to open the university's new chemical laboratory; Dora Marsden was arrested. Five days later there was a militant demonstration when Lloyd George visited Newcastle; stones were thrown at a car in which he was thought to be travelling. Twelve women were imprisoned – two, Lady Constance Lytton and Jane Brailsford, received preferential treatment. Jane, a WSPU member and a former member of the NUWSS, was the wife of the journalist H. N. Brailsford, already mentioned; he had long been a staunch advocate of women's suffrage, and, since the summer of 1909, he had been doing his best to try and convince the Liberal Government either to give time for the passage of a moderate suffrage Bill which would get the support of all parties or to seek an electoral mandate to extend the franchise to women. The arrest of his wife further strengthened Brailsford's sympathies with the suffrage movement. He was appalled by the Government's brutal treatment of those arrested and full of admiration for the courage and determination of the militants, writing in a private letter: 'I am not a woman's man. I am indeed quite unsusceptible save in my wife's case. But towards all of these twelve, from the brave little mill girl to Lady Constance Lytton – a saintly woman – I feel a reverence I could not exaggerate.'

Winston Churchill was a favourite target; very few of his meetings were free of suffragette disturbance. In Dundee, his home constituency, five suffragettes disrupted a meeting in October; they were Adela Pankhurst, Helen Archdale, Maud

Joachim, Catherine Corbett and Lara Evans. Their protest led to the inevitable arrests, followed by prison sentences, followed by hunger strikes.

Several women appeared in court in Bristol in connection with his visit to the city. Theresa Garnett threatened him with a whip when he got off his train at Temple Meads station, calling out, 'You Brute! You Brute! I will show you what Englishwomen can do.' Asked to give her name to the authorities, she responded, 'My name is "Votes for Women" and my home is anywhere!' She was charged with assault but this was reduced to one of disturbing the peace. She was bound over to keep the peace for six months, and told to find two sureties or go to prison; she chose the latter course. Another suffragette, Jessie Laws, had thrown stones at the Colston Hall from the top of a tram while Churchill was dining there. Mary Allen and Vera Wentworth served fourteen days for breaking windows during the visit. On their release, both said they had been forcibly fed and made to put on prison clothes. They revealed that other women had been forcibly fed; Theresa Garnett had set fire to her cell in protest at her treatment.

On 4 December, four women appeared in court at Preston, also charged with offences relating to a visit by Churchill. One was Mrs Massy from Kensington, who had thrown a stone through the window of the post office. It was wrapped in a paper which bore the words, 'This stone through the window of the Hall is to remind you of your broken pledges made to the suffragists of Manchester and Dundee.' In the end she did not throw it through the Hall window in case someone was hurt. She was fined 20s, with £2 damages, or one month in prison. Three local women were charged with resisting the police; Catherine Worthington, Elizabeth Hesmondhalgh and Edith Rigby were each fined 5s with cost, or seven days in gaol. Edith's father was typical of many fathers in thinking evil women had led his daughter astray; he claimed that she had 'fallen into the hands of hired women who made a profitable investment out of her'. In fact, she was acting very much on principle, as her later career was to show.

All these were intended as dramatic gestures; it was never intended to physically hurt anybody. Of course the Government could not be sure of this; there were many wild rumours of planned assassinations of Government ministers. This would have been anathema to the Pankhursts, but it was always possible that some so-called 'supporter' might resort to such an extreme action, so the authorities had to be cautious. Even Churchill's young baby, Diana, received police protection when she was pushed around the park; this was ridiculed in *Votes for Women* and one suffragette branch sent her a doll to show their goodwill – dressed in suffragette colours of course!

In the event, the one case where a suffragette stunt may have caused harm to anyone other than the perpetrator was at the Bermondsey by-election of 28 October 1909. The Women's Freedom League determined that, as no woman could vote in the election, they would cause it to be declared void; they would do this by destroying some of the ballot papers. Two of their members, Alison Neilans and Alice Chapin, an American, undertook the task. Each carried a test tube containing ink and chemicals, and each entered a polling booth and smashed the test tube against the box in order to pour the liquid into the box and destroy the papers inside. As women could not vote, their presence in the booths aroused the suspicions of the (male) authorities, who rushed to stop them; some of the liquid from Mrs Chapin's test tube splashed into the eye of one of the men, a Mr Thorley.

Inevitably both sides had their own take on the incident; the *Pall Mall Gazette* called it an 'outrage unparalleled in English history'. Anti-suffragists claimed that Thorley could easily have been blinded, and he certainly wore a patch over his eye for some time afterwards, but supporters of the campaign claimed he was faking his injury – they had called at his house one evening without notice and he was not wearing the patch! It turned out that the slight damage to his eye had not been caused by chemicals in the test tube, but by ammonia Thorley had applied to his injury. Both women had been sentenced to three months for the destruction of ballot papers, and Alice Chapin to a further four months for the assault; she was granted the king's pardon for the latter 'offence', so that both served merely the three months for criminal damage. The suffragettes' pledge to harm nobody still held.

October 1909 saw yet another form of protest, with the formation of the Women's Tax Resistance League. Women from all three main groups, and many others, drew on an old tradition in England of refusal to pay taxes, arguing that women without votes were illegally taxed by Parliament. Historically minded campaigners took their inspiration from earlier protests on similar lines; a favourite was John Hampden's refusal to pay ship money to King Charles I in the 1640s. It had already been used in the campaign for women's suffrage. Dora Montefiore refused to pay tax in 1904 and 1905, and in 1906 went a stage further, barricading herself in her house to keep out the bailiff. Annie Kenney and Teresa Billington brought fifty women in support, in what became known as the 'Siege of Fort Montefiore'. Her goods were eventually distrained and sold at public auction; she bought them back herself.

The WSPU had begun resisting the payment of income tax in 1907, and the WFL began to urge 'no vote – no tax' in the same year. In January 1908, Charlotte Despard saw it as one part of a larger general strike of women, which would extend to the refusal to bear children, to manage their homes, or to fulfil any of the citizen duties which they currently performed. Anne Cobden Sanderson now turned primarily to the tactic of tax resistance, helping to set the league up and speaking widely on its behalf until it suspended activities in August 1914; more than 220 women participated between 1906 and 1918. The women were content to pay local taxes because women could vote for local councils, but they would not pay national taxes – property tax, income tax and licensing fees such as those for dogs, cars and carriages, and guns.

Some of these women were very wealthy – Charlotte Despard was the heiress to the Knight's Castile soap fortune. The Government seized goods from those who refused to pay tax and auctioned them, and in the case of the richest women this led to a great deal of very welcome publicity. A Rembrandt painting was taken from a Miss MacGregor of Arbroath and sold for just £75! Others who had property seized included Dr Ethel Williams, the Duchess of Bedford, whose goods were distrained in 1913, and Princess Sophia Duleep Singh; the latter had a diamond ring seized in 1910 and a pearl necklace and gold bangle in 1914, the latter being auctioned in Twickenham Town Hall. Supporters often attended these auctions, bought the items and gave them back: Charlotte Despard's piano was sold and bought back several times, becoming a standing joke!

The refusal to pay dog licenses reached the less wealthy, especially as richer dog owners were sometimes passed over; Sophia Duleep Singh had eight dogs but was never pursued for not buying licences for them. In sharp contrast, a working-class supporter, Emma Sproson, who refused to pay her dog license, was imprisoned twice at Stafford for a total of six weeks. The magistrate ordered her to serve her time in the third division, and had to be reminded that she should have at least been placed in the second. In the event, Emma went on hunger strike until she was moved into the first division. Her dog was shot by the police, an unlikely martyr to the suffragette cause.

It was also in 1909 that the NUWSS made clear its disapproval of militant methods. The NUWSS council passed a resolution which condemned the use of violence and distributed copies of the statement to all Members of Parliament and to the press: 'The Council of the National Union of Women's Suffrage Societies strongly condemns the use of violence in political propaganda and, being convinced that the way of advancing the cause of women's suffrage is by energetic, law-abiding propaganda, reaffirms its adherence to constitutional principles.' At their 1909 annual meeting, the suffragists again emphasised their determination to separate themselves from the WSPU by passing a resolution which required all members of the society to pledge to support only 'lawful and constitutional methods' and to accept the NUWSS by-election policy.

By the end of 1909 the goodwill between the NUWSS and the WSPU had largely vanished. However, the contrast between the two groups can be taken too far; as even Millicent Fawcett noted:

> Far more violence was suffered by the Suffragettes than they inflicted on their opponents ... I must mention here what I myself have seen, and a sickening and terrible sight it was: suffragettes being carried by main force out of an Albert Hall meeting; a girl violently struggling, but powerless in the clutches of four men, two to her shoulders and two to her feet, and while in this defenceless position violently smitten on the face by enraged members of the Liberal Party: both fists and umbrellas were used in this cowardly assault.

It was not just hecklers who suffered violence; women risked physical assault simply by holding meetings. Mary Blathwayt gave a speech from a lorry in Bristol in 1909: 'I was hit by potatoes, stones, turf and dust. Something hit me very hard on my right ear as I was getting into our tram. Someone threw a big stone as big as a baby's head; it fell onto my lorry.'

The 'outrages' of the WSPU brought the issue of women's rights continually into the public eye – as they were intended to do. This made women think about the issue, and led them to want to involve themselves in the cause, even if not within the WSPU. In November 1909, Lady Frances Balfour, one of the highest members of the British aristocracy to devote herself to the suffragette cause, spoke to the Edinburgh Circle of the Conservative and Unionist Women's Franchise Association. She said that she would have nothing to do with militant tactics – but she did not think that such tactics would kill the suffrage movement: 'They had made people like her feel that the time had come when those who were in favour of the enfranchisement of women could no longer sit with hands folded and let others fight the battle. If they disapproved of the militant tactics it was for them to come forward and win in other ways.'

1. 'Torturing Women in Prison'. (Amberley Archive)

2. NUWSS poster appealing for votes for women on the same terms as men. (Norfolk Record Office)

3. 'Handicapped': poster designed by Duncan Grant. (Author's Collection)

4. 'Convicts, lunatics and women have no vote'. (Amberley Archive)

5. Poster for the NUWSS March, 1908. (Author's Collection)

6. Poster aimed at working-class women. (Author's Collection)

Above: 7. Pankhurst scathingly portrayed as goose giving speech to the gaggle regarding votes for women. (June Purvis)

Left: 8. Illustration shows five women suffragettes, wearing Napoleonic hats and great coats, standing on a tiny island. (Amberley Archive)

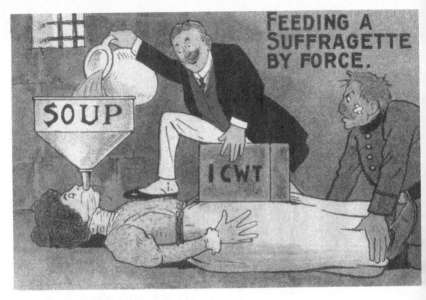

Above: 9. 'Feeding a suffragette by force'. (June Purvis)

Below left: 10. Violent means of getting rid of suffragettes are suggested. (June Purvis)

Below right: 11. Pankhurst portrayed mocking a man. (June Purvis)

A peep into the Future
House of (un)Commons

Meeting of Cabinet Ministers 1978.
MRS SPANKHURST, M.P., DELIVERING HER MAIDEN SPEECH.

Above: 12. Comic portrayal of women behaving in a variety of irrational ways as MPs within Parliament. (June Purvis)

Left: 13. Comic portrayal of women sitting around taking tea as a cabinet meeting. (June Purvis)

14. Woman portrayed as annoying and bossy wife. (June Purvis)

15. Postcard mocking women at a suffragette meeting implying that all suffragettes are ugly. (June Purvis)

16. Death at the Derby I. (Author's Collection)

17. Suffragette leaders (from left, as we look at the picture): Constance Lytton, Annie Kenney, Emmeline Pethick-Lawrence, Christabel Pankhurst, Sylvia Pankhurst. (Author's Collection)

18. Contrasting uniforms: Edith How Martyn as university lecturer and as Holloway prisoner. (Amberley Archive)

Above: 19. The argument of the stone. (Author's Collection)

Above right: 20. Charlotte Despard, of the Women's Freedom League. (Amberley Archive)

Below right: 21. Mrs Emmeline Pankhurst. (Amberley Archive)

Above: 22. Miss Christabel Pankhurst.
(Author's Collection)

Left: 23. 'Votes For Women'.
(Author's Collection)

24. Arrest! (Amberley Archive)

25. Suffragettes of all ages at a meeting in London. (Amberley Archive)

26. Emmeline Pankhurst campaigns at a by-election. (Author's Collection)

Above right: 27. Emmeline and Christabel Pankhurst in prison dress. (Author's Collection)

Above left: 28. Protesting women are turned away by the police. (Author's Collection)

Below left: 29. 'Window Breaking and Incitement to Mutiny'. (Author's Collection)

Hampstead Women's Social and Political Union,
178, FINCHLEY ROAD, N.W.

WINDOW BREAKING

AND

INCITEMENT

TO

MUTINY.

For Breaking Windows as a Political protest, Women are now in H.M. Gaols serving sentences of
Four and Six months Imprisonment.

For Inciting Soldiers to Disobey Orders, a much more serious crime, known to the law as a felony, and punishable by penal servitude, the Publishers of the "Syndicalist," were sentenced to nine months hard labour, and the Printers of the paper to six months hard labour.

The Government under the pressure of men with votes reduced this sentence on the Publishers to
Six months imprisonment without hard labour.

and the sentence on the Printers to
One month without hard labour.

IS THIS JUSTICE TO VOTELESS WOMEN ?

30. Empty mansion at St Leonard's set alight by Kitty Marion in April 1913. (Author's Collection)

31. Flora Drummond and Emmeline and Sylvia Pankhurst arrested by Inspector Jarvis a the WSPU offices. (Author's Collection)

Above: 32. Suffragettes in London picketing for women's suffrage. (Amberley Archive)

Left: 33. Six-frame cartoon showing obese English suffragette in prison being served a lot of food by John Bull, but refusing to eat. She becomes very thin and is pulled through bars by other suffragettes. (Amberley Archive)

Above: 34. Suffragette graduates protest. (Author's Collection)

Right: 35. Suffragette throwing a bag of flour at Mr Asquith in Chester. (Author's Collection)

Below: 36. Princess Sophia Duleep Singh outside Hampton Court Palace. (Author's Collection)

37. Suffragettes on the march in 1910: the arrows indicate those who have been in prison for the cause. (Author's Collection)

38. Avoiding the census, 1911: these women are sleeping in an 'unoccupied' house. (Author's Collection)

Above: 39. Davison's funeral procession. (Author's Collection)

Right: 40. Suffragette as Joan of Arc. (Author's Collection)

Above: 41. The Britannia Pier, Great Yarmouth, set on fire by suffragettes 17 April 1914. (Norfolk Record Office, Y/TPL 3/2)

Left: 42. Saunderton railway station, Buckinghamshire, after an arson attack by suffragettes, March 1913. (Amberley Archive)

43. The Tea House at Kew Gardens, London, burnt down by Lily Lenton and Olive Wharry in February 1913. (Amberley Archive)

Right: 44. Suffragette and feminist Sybil Margaret Thomas, Viscountess Rhondda (1857–1941), with her husband Welsh industrialist and politician David Alfred Thomas, 1st Viscount Rhondda (1856–1918), who served as British munitions commissioner. (Amberley Archive)

Below: 45. Death at the Derby II. (Author's Collection)

Left: 46. Miriam Pratt protests in Norwich, 1913. (*Eastern Daily Press*)

Below: 47. Outside Buckingham palace. (Author's Collection)

48. Poster aimed at
working-class women.
(Amberley Archive)

49. Wartime devotion.
(Author's Collection)

50. At last – the first female member of Parliament, Lady Nancy Astor. (Author's Collection)

51. 'Justice Demands the Vote': poster issued by the Brighton and Hove Society for Women's Suffrage and promoted by the Artists' Suffrage League. (Norfolk Record Office)

6

1910: The Conciliation Bill and 'Black Friday'

In January 1910, Lady Lytton deliberately had herself arrested at a suffragette demonstration; her aim was to prove that upper-class women did receive preferential treatment. This time she told the police her name was Jane Warton and that she was a seamstress. As a result when she went on hunger strike, she was not tested for heart problems, and she was forcibly fed eight times before her release. It was the account that she gave of the horrors of force-feeding that brought the practice into the public eye. She wrote,

I had been in this movement many months, and although I absolutely approved of the method of getting in our messages by means of stones which did nothing but convey our meaning to the Ministers and to the world, still I felt I could not throw a stone myself. However, as I have told you before, when I saw the first of these women released – a mere girl – from Birmingham Gaol, I took another view. I went to Newcastle for a protest, meaning to share what these women endured. I went in my own name, and as you know, I was released after a very short hunger-strike, a heart specialist being called in, who examined me for something like a quarter of an hour. I made a tremendous protest. I said that in that same prison where I was, there was a woman, a first offender, who had done much less violence than I had, and she was fed by force without having her heart tested at all. 'Whatever you think of the subject,' I said, 'whatever you think of the militant movement, surely you can see that justice is done between one human being and another!' I tried all I could, when I came out, and I got others whom I knew to fight that question with truth and exposure, and what did they give us back?

Lies, and nothing but lies!

Well, I thought, you choose your weapons. I will fight with the same weapon, and you shall take my life, and do with it what you will! So I disguised myself; I changed my personality, and I went and made my protest outside that very gaol where these hideous, abominable things were being done. It was easier than I thought. I merely cut my hair. I bought clothes of a different type to my own, I removed initials from my underclothes, I put on glasses, and that was more than sufficient. I had one rather unhappy moment. They had taken my belongings, brooches, handkerchief, etc. I saw in the first bundle a reel of cotton with 'Lytton' on it, and a handkerchief from which I had omitted to remove the initials. I thought that the game was up but they were so little suspicious that I simply placed my hand upon these two things and put them into the fire. The prison world is so used to suffragettes doing strange things that they were not at all surprised.

I was always on the alert for being discovered, but the first day of the hunger strike went by, the second day went by, and the third day went by, and it was quite obvious from the way they treated me they did not suspect my identity. It was the first time I had been to prison without my name, and I can assure you it made a great deal of difference. Perhaps it is only human. I do not complain of position influencing people like wardresses or policemen, but when it comes to law and the Home Office surely one can expect something more like justice! On the fourth day of my hunger-strike the doctor came to my cell and said he must feed me at once. I was so desirous of gaining my object – I knew that if I was only fed once, it would be a test – that I did not look upon it with horror – I welcomed it. To my surprise and to my great relief, they did not examine my heart, which I had managed for two days, but which by the fourth day of starvation was becoming difficult.

At last they came. It is like describing a hospital scene – and much worse. The doctor and four wardresses came into my cell. I decided to save all my resistance for the actual feeding, and when they pointed to my bed on the floor, I lay down, and the doctor did not even feel my pulse. Two wardresses held my hands, one my head. Much as I had heard about this thing, it was infinitely more horrible and more painful than I had expected. The doctor put the steel gag in somewhere on my gums and forced my mouth till it was yawning wide. As he proceeded to force into my mouth and down the throat a large rubber tube, I felt as though I were being killed – absolute suffocation is the feeling. You feel as though it would never stop. You cannot stop. You cannot breathe, and yet you choke. It irritates the throat, it irritates the mucous membrane as it goes down, every second seems an hour, and you think they will never finish pushing it down. After a while the sensation is relieved, then the food poured down, and then again you choke, and your whole body resists and writhes under the treatment; you are held down, and the process goes on, and finally, when the vomiting becomes excessive, the tube is removed. I forgot what I was in there for, I forgot women, I forget everything except my own sufferings, and I was completely overcome by them.

What was even worse to me than the thing itself was the positive terror with which I anticipated its renewal. Very soon I thought to try and appeal to that man as a doctor to perform an operation in a better way, but whatever one said or suggested was treated with most absolute contempt.

There was one even worse thing, and that was the moral poisoning if one may call it that, of one's whole mind. I always closed my eyes. I tried not to see the beings who came to do this thing. I felt it was too hideous, and I did not wish it imprinted on my eyes. Nevertheless I got to hate those men and women, I got to hate infinitely more the powers that stood behind them, I got to hate the blindness, the prejudice, in those who turn away and won't look or listen to what is being done under their very eyes. I tried to think of the splendid heroes and heroines since the world began, of all the martyrs, all the magnificent women in this movement, and I felt a tremendous gratitude to them, an admiration which overpowered me. But it was no use to me – it did not help me and it did not strengthen me.

The Lytton case demonstrates the sense of solidarity felt within the suffragette movement: Elsie Howey broke the prison governor's windows, and was also gaoled, in order that Lady Constance should not suffer alone. Constance Lytton felt this made Elsie the 'most dear one of our members'. There was undoubtedly a bonding experience among suffragettes, formed by their common experiences. Lady Lytton herself referred to 'that full unfettered companionship which is among the greatest immediate rewards of those who work actively in this cause'.

Constance Lytton herself had this to say about her actions:

People say 'What does this hunger-strike mean? Surely it is all folly. If it is not hysteria at least it is unreasonable.' They will not realise that we are like an army, that we are deputed to fight for a cause, and for other people, and in any struggle or any fight weapons must be used. The weapons for which we ask are simple – a fair hearing; but that is refused us in Parliament, refused us by the Government, refused us in the magistrates' courts, refused us in the law courts. Then we must have other weapons. What do other people choose when they are driven to the last extremity? What do men choose? They have recourse to violence. But what the women of this movement have specially stood out for, is that they will not kill, they will not harm, while they have other weapons left them. These women have chosen the weapon of self-hurt to make their protest, and this hunger-strike brings great pressure upon the Government. It involves grave hurt and tremendous sacrifice, but this is on the part of the women only, and does not physically injure their enemies. Can that be called violence and hooliganism?

Lady Lytton never fully recovered from the ordeal she had been through; she had a heart attack in August 1910, and in 1912 suffered a stroke that left her paralysed.

Suffragettes went on hunger strike in Ireland too. Here, the hunger strike had long been used as a political weapon from medieval times, but the Irish suffragettes were the first prisoners to go on hunger-strike for their political rights in the twentieth century. One was Hanna Sheehy-Skeffington, a teacher who had founded the Irish Women's Franchise League in 1908. In 1913, she was imprisoned for stone-throwing at Dublin Castle, and went on hunger strike. In Ireland, rights for women were intermixed with demands for independence from Britain: Hanna's husband was shot dead by a British soldier during the Easter Rising of 1916. In her pamphlet *Reminiscences of an Irish Suffragette*, she pointed out, 'Hunger-strike was then a new weapon – we were the first to try it out in Ireland – had we but known, we were the pioneers in a long line. At first, Sinn Fein and its allies regarded the hunger-strike as a womanish thing.' Irish republicans soon adopted the hunger strike as a weapon, culminating in the mass action of 1981; this time there was no force-feeding, and the men were allowed to die.

There was a general election in January 1910; the suffragettes naturally seized the opportunity to hold rallies and meetings throughout the country, and to stage demonstrations outside polling booths on election day. The ever-present risk of physical violence from men opposed to their cause came to a head at Southport where three suffragettes – Mary Gawthorpe, Dora Marsden and Mabel Capper – were badly beaten up. The three brought charges for assault against three men, but the magistrate dismissed the case.

In the event, the Liberal Government was returned with a much reduced majority. After the general election, a group of MPs from all parties (but mostly Liberals) put forward a Conciliation Bill. A committee was formed to draft a women's suffrage Bill; its members included Lord Lytton and H. N. Brailsford. This put forward a proposal which would give the vote to all women who occupied property in their own right – in effect, to many single women, about 1 million of whom would receive the vote under the scheme. It did not exclude married women, but made clear that husband and wife could not both qualify on the grounds of owning the same property; in effect, those women who would be able to vote if the Bill became law were very much those who could already vote in local elections. On 14 February, suffragettes declared a truce while this Bill went through Parliament. Christabel Pankhurst spoke to a rally of 40,000 women in London: 'We have at any rate got an assurance which will place in our hands before the next election the right to vote.'

The Conciliation Bill was introduced into Parliament on 14 June by David Shackleton, Labour MP for Clitheroe; the main women's groups gave their support in their own ways. The NUWSS sponsored a meeting to support the Bill while the WSPU organised a march of 15,000 women in a 2-mile-long procession from the Embankment to Albert Hall. This took place on 18 June. Preparations were announced in advance:

The Women Suffrage procession, which is to march this evening from the Thames Embankment to the Albert Hall, will form up on the Embankment at 6.30. Owing to its great length, it has been necessary to arrange the procession in two main portions – one extending to Westminster Bridge and the other to Blackfriars Bridge. These will face each other across Northumberland Avenue. Another section will be drawn up in Whitehall and a fourth in Victoria Street. Altogether the procession will consist of seven sections, four of them being made up almost entirely of those members of the WSPU who are not walking with the graduates', writers', artists' or nurses' groups. The other sections will represent the different suffrage societies.

The officials in charge of the procession will consist of a 'General' on horseback (Mrs Drummond), a chief marshal (Miss Jessie Kenney), a chief banner marshal (Miss Irene Dallas), and two mounted marshals (the Hon. Mrs Haverfield and Miss Vera Holme). Each section will be in the charge of a section marshal, a banner marshal, and a certain number of group 'captains' and banner 'captains', making in all sixty-one officials, in addition to several hundred bearers.

The route taken will be along Northumberland Avenue, Cockspur Street, Pall Mall, St James's Street, Piccadilly, Knightsbridge Road and Kensington Road. The march will begin at 6.30 to the music of forty bands, headed by the drum and fife band of the WSPU.

Most women thought that victory was in sight at last, which made the subsequent disappointment even more bitter.

On 25 June 1910, *The Times* published an article, 'The

Present Strength of the Woman Suffrage Movement', which summarised what had been achieved so far:

An important sign of activity during the last four or five years has been the growth of suffrage societies. Not only have the older societies increased enormously in strength since the end of 1905, but 18 new associations have sprung into existence. before that date there were only three of any importance, the NUWSS (including affiliated associations), the WSPU which had then been working in Manchester on non-militant lines, for something like two years, and the Lancashire and Cheshire Women's Suffrage Society, originally an association of women textile workers, now a society with a more extended sphere of influence, as is implied in its new name – the National Industrial and Professional Women's Suffrage Society (secretary Miss Esther Roper) and still independent of the NUWSS, though non-militant in method.

Since 1905, political women, University women, and professional women of all kinds have banded themselves together in suffrage unions; while men and women, men alone, and boys and girls have severally done the same.

NUWSS: the oldest woman suffrage organization in the kingdom, and has a fine historic record behind it of steady constitutional effort, maintaining through many years when women's suffrage was still outside the realm of practical politics. An important branch of its work has been the organisation of suffrage societies, of which 119 are now affiliated to the union, a number which does not include local branches, in many cases flourishing societies in themselves, which bring up the total to 183 ... All the affiliated societies and their branches are pledged to the non-party, non-militant policy of the national Union, and agitate for the suffrage by all the ordinary methods, by holding large meetings – the Albert Hall has been filled more than once – by dissembling literature, interviewing Ministers etc. The NUWSS organised the first procession of voteless women, known as the 'mud march' in February 1907, since when it has been responsible for others of a similar kind.

The National WSPU is a militant suffrage society, having initiated and adopted forcible tactics in October 1905, when Miss Christabel Pankhurst, their originator and the present organizing secretary of the union, suffered imprisonment with Miss Annie Kenney for holding a meeting and causing obstruction in the street after being ejected from Sir Edward Grey's meeting in the Free Trade Hall, Manchester. Subsequent imprisonment of members of the NWSPU have been consequent upon demonstrations in Parliament Square, when deputations of women were refused admission to the House of Commons, and upon demonstrations outside political meetings in the provinces, from which the women were excluded on account of their known determination to utter a protest, whenever a Cabinet minister was speaking, against the inactivity of the Government in dealing with their question. The NWSPU was the first society to adopt this anti-Government policy; and it consistently opposes the Government nominee at all Parliamentary elections, preserving a strict neutrality with regard to other candidates; and it will continue to do so as long as the Government in power refuses to enfranchise women.

At the time of writing, a truce has been called in the

militant tactics of the NWSPU, and a vigorous educational campaign is being carried on all over the country. Ever since its foundation, however, propaganda work has formed the larger if less noticeable part of the union's activities. It will be remembered that this organisation held the great Hyde Park demonstration of June 1908; it holds meetings in the Albert Hall three or four times a year, besides thousands of others all over the country, by means of a network of organisations working from twenty-three centres outside the metropolis. The NWSPU is remarkable for the amount of money it raises, its campaign fund having risen from £29,000 to £61,000 in the year ended February 1910.

The Women's Freedom League is the second militant suffrage society in existence. It has a democratic constitution and possesses sixty-four local branches. While refraining from making protests at Cabinet ministers' meetings, it pursues the anti-Government policy at by-elections, and numbers of its members have suffered terms of imprisonment for making protests in the Ladies' Gallery, in Parliament Square, and in Downing Street. In order to demonstrate the right of petition, members of the WFL picketed the House of Commons for sixteen weeks last autumn, throughout the duration of every sitting of the house. This league was the first association to hold a suffrage bazaar, two years ago; and its Yule-tide festival in the Albert Hall last December was the latest of its kind. Like the two unions already named, it makes a special feature of its literature department, and a complete education in suffrage matters can be obtained by an exhaustive study of the books and pamphlets issued by all three.

On 11/12 July a majority of MPs voted in favour of the Conciliation Bill, which was referred to a Committee of Whole House. However, in November Parliament was dissolved because of differences between the House of Lords and the Commons on financial issues. The suffragettes tried to gain assurance from the Prime Minister of the future of the Conciliation Bill, but he refused to meet their deputations. The WSPU truce ended on 18 November, a day known to history as 'Black Friday'. Suffragettes trying to reach Parliament were met with violence and brutality from police, plain-clothes men and male onlookers. Ada Wright recalled what happened:

When we reached Parliament Square, plain-clothes men mingling with the crowd kicked us, and added to the horror and anguish of the day by dragging some of our women down side streets. There were many attempts of indecent assault.

The police rode at us with shire horses, so I caught hold of the reins of one of the horses and would not let go. A policeman grabbed my arm and twisted it round and round until I felt the bone almost breaking and I sank to the pavement, helpless. A contingent of the United States Navy was in London at the time, and they lined up outside Westminster Abbey and watched the proceedings. I was continually tripped up by the police and thrown to the ground in the sight of the American sailors. Each time I got up, and once more made a show of advancing to the House of Commons only to be thrown to the ground once again ...

As I leaned against the railings after one of these episodes, a sense of the humiliation I was undergoing came over me. I wondered what my relations would think of me if they were to see me. When night came, I was mercifully arrested. After a long proceeding in the police station, we were bailed out and I returned to where I was staying at one o'clock in the morning. As I lay down, tired and exhausted, I said to myself with a shudder, 'What a sordid day.'

The next morning I found I had been photographed lying on the ground where I had been flung, and the photograph occupied the front page of the *Daily Mirror*. As soon as this became known to the Government, an order to have the picture suppressed was sent to the offices of the newspaper, but they could not suppress the copies which had been sold. There were headlines: BLACK FRIDAY.

Women were thrown from one policeman to another who punched them with fists, striking women in their faces, breasts and shoulders. Georgiana Solomon was so badly hurt that she was confined to bed for a month. As soon as she was well enough, she complained to the Home Office; when nothing was done, she published her letter in *The Times*:

The methods applied to us were those used by the police to conquer the pugilistic antagonist, to fell the burglar, to maim the hooligan, or to reduce to inanity the semi-barbaric and dangerous rough ... When walking down the road I found myself in danger of being knocked down, and endeavoured to regain a place on the pavement, but had scarcely secured a footing when a policeman made a rush at me ... He held and violently shook me while his helpers twirled round my arms as if to drag them from their sockets. Still worse, another caught me by the shoulders and mercilessly pressed his heavy weight upon my back, crushing me down, while he propelled me along the line, uniformed men assisting.

Another suffragette to suffer brutality was Rosa May Billinghurst. Disabled from an early age, she went to the demonstration in a specially adapted tricycle; she was thrown from the vehicle and arrested.

Emmeline Pankhurst was not among the 115 women and 4 men arrested but saw with horror the treatment meted out to the women, who later told her, 'We cannot bear this'; indeed, for many women window-breaking, which resulted in immediate arrest, was beginning to seem a 'safer' form of militancy.

Three women died as a result of their injuries that day. First was Mary Clarke, Emmeline Pankhurst's sister. She was imprisoned in Holloway for a month, being released shortly before Christmas. According to Antonia Raeburn, two days after her prison release, Mrs Clarke was spending Christmas day with the Pankhursts, when she complained of feeling tired and left the family party to lie down. When Mrs Pankhurst went upstairs to see her sister some time later, she found her dead; the shock of the events of the previous month had been too much for her. She was described in *Votes for Women* as 'the first woman martyr who has gone to death for this cause'.

The following week, a second victim of Black Friday, Henria Williams, died of heart failure. Henria made a statement saying what had happened:

> One policeman after knocking me about for some considerable time, finally took hold of me with his great strong hand like iron just over my heart. He hurt me so much that at first I had not the voice power to tell him what he was doing. But I knew that unless I made a strong effort to do so he would kill me. So collecting all the power of my being, I commanded him to take his hand off my heart ... Yet that policeman would not arrest me and he was the third or fourth who had knocked me about.

She was not exaggerating; she never recovered, and died of a heart attack just two months after it. Another victim was Cecilia Haig, who was severely assaulted and trampled; she was nursed by her sister but died a year later, in December 1911. *Votes For Women* blamed her death on the treatment she had received on Black Friday.

Black Friday was a terrifying display of the physical force that male opposition could inflict. Susan Kingsley Kent has called it 'an unprecedented display of male brutality ... for six hours the women suffered "violent and indecent treatment" at the hands of police and bystanders ... the attacks on the women were explicitly sexual'. The accusation of sexual attack had appeared within a month of the attack, in Georgiana Solomon's letter: 'I may add that I was gripped by the breast – by no means an exceptional act, for heart-breaking to relate, I am medically informed that younger women, women of an age to be my own daughters, were also assaulted in this and other repellent and equally cruel ways.'

Four days after Black Friday, Emmeline Pankhurst was speaking at Caxton Hall when a message reached her that Asquith had made a vague statement hinting that a Bill could come before the House of Commons that could then be amended by MPs. She immediately marched to Downing Street with her supporters to protest at the indecisive nature of this statement. Violent struggles broke out between the women and the police. This time Emmeline was among the 156 arrested but since no evidence was offered against her, she was discharged. In her special message to the members of the Black Friday and Downing Street demonstrations, she praised the 'magnificent courage and self-restraint' the women had shown and humbly confessed, 'I feel myself deeply honoured to be your leader.'

London and Lancashire have always been thought the rightful homes of the suffragette movement, but there were active women all around the country. Yorkshire was another area where working-class mill girls took up the cause, mainly through the WSPU, led by Adela Pankhurst, until she withdrew from the campaign in 1912 after her health had broken down. The women were campaigning both for the vote and for better pay and conditions in their factories and mills; tailoress Lavena Saltonstall, who led a weavers' strike in Hebden Bridge, even persuaded Emmeline Pankhurst to visit the town to support the strike. She stood on the steps of Bridge Mill on 28 January 1907, addressing the strikers. Four days later, after Emmeline had gone, the women marched to the houses of the employers. Stones were thrown at windows and two women, Jessie Baines and Laura Wilson, were fined; refusing to pay, they were sent to prison.

Other mill girls went to London to take part in 'outrages' there, such as Dora Thewlis, who was only sixteen when she was arrested outside Parliament Square. The London magistrates commented that she ought to have been still at school, not appreciating that, like many thousands of others, Dora had been working in a mill since she was thirteen years old. The story was another propaganda coup, making the front page of the *Daily Mirror*: Dora became known as the 'baby suffragette'. Another woman from the Yorkshire WSPU to make her mark was Lilian Lenton, a dancer, who, on her twenty-first birthday, vowed to set fire to two empty buildings a week until the women got the vote. She almost died during a hunger strike in 1913, when the feeding tube was wrongly inserted into her lungs. The Home Secretary denied that any food had gone into her lungs, but three doctors wrote to *The Times* stating that this was the case and that it had caused a condition, which, 'but for her youth and good, healthy physique would have ended more seriously'. Another Yorkshire suffragette was Mary Gawthorpe, a teacher who worked full-time for the WSPU in Leeds from 1906; in 1909 she was badly beaten after heckling Winston Churchill at a meeting. There *were* some middle-class members of the Yorkshire WSPU, but most higher-status women preferred the NUWSS, such as Isabella Ford of Leeds, a former member of the WSPU whose support for the Labour Party led her into the NUWSS, and Florence

Lockwood, the wife of Josiah Lockwood, a manufacturer in Colne Valley.

Working-class girls in the North were drawn into the struggle because suffrage was debated in meetings of their trade unions and in the Women's Co-operative Guild. This was built on by the North of England Women's Suffrage Society; its leaders, Esther Roper and Eva Gore Booth, worked with local working-class women like Sarah Reddish, Sarah Dickenson and Selina Cooper to gather signatures on petitions; Reddish and Cooper were among the women who had presented the petition to the House of Commons in 1901. The trade unions gradually pushed ahead of the society, organising meetings through its branches. Some suffragists found the WSPU too radical in its approach, but in some cities like Liverpool the WSPU remained a major force, with a strong support among the working class; the local branch had been founded by Mrs Morissey, helped by Patricia Woodlock, the daughter of a house-painter, and Emma Hillier, a dress-maker. Women who did not want to go down the full militant path could still take part by daubing slogans and holding public meetings; working-class women, poorly educated, sometimes lacked the self-confidence to speak at the latter – but there were plenty of exceptions, such as Annie Kenney! Others could help with the very necessary fund-raising. When Ada Flatman became WSPU organiser in Liverpool in 1912, she opened a WSPU shop: Emmeline Pethick-Lawrence, as the national treasurer, was doubtful about the new enterprise, but in its first year it raised £592 for the cause.

There were some working-class suffragettes in other parts of Britain, combining the demand for the vote with concerns about wages and working conditions. They included Alice Hawkins, who worked among the boot- and shoe-makers in Leicester, and Elizabeth Andrews and Rose Davies in the South Wales coalfields. If the suffrage movement appears to be largely a middle- or even upper-class movement, this is very much as viewed from London; across the country, women of all classes were very much involved, but of course a working woman would not have the time to devote to the cause that a woman of independent means would.

Some women in the trade union movement thought that advancing women's working conditions was a more important issue than suffrage. They included Margaret Bondfield, who, according to Sylvia Pankhurst, 'deprecated votes for women as the hobby of old maids whom no-one wanted to marry'. Dorothy Jewson of Norwich was in both camps, campaigning for the WSPU before the war and then working in the union movement. These two and another trade union activist, Susan Lawrence, were to become three early women MPs in 1923. The two approaches were not mutually exclusive: both strands of action helped in the empowerment of women.

7
1911: The Failure of Conciliation

The suffragettes resumed their truce in honour of Coronation year. On 21 January, Dr Ethel Smyth gave the first performance of her newly composed 'March of the Women' and presented the piece to Emmeline Pankhurst. The words were written by Cicely Hamilton, an actress and playwright who was also a strong supporter of women's rights. Music played a large part in the movement; there were bands in the processions and the meetings, and sometimes suffragettes would gather outside a prison and sing in support of their comrades inside; on one occasion, Flora Drummond danced a highland fling outside Holloway Prison. Mary Leigh often acted as drum major for the drum and fife band which accompanied many WSPU processions.

There were a large number of actresses in the suffrage movement, and they had their own grouping, the Actresses' Franchise League. Many were also in the WSPU, like Vera Holme, a member of the chorus of the D'Oyly Carte Opera Company, who became Mrs Pankhurst's driver after a supporter had donated the money to buy her a car.

The 1911 Census

On 2 April many suffragettes boycotted the national census. This was a WFL idea, one of their most dramatic acts of passive resistance, but the WSPU were also enthusiastic. The organisers provided a form: 'If I am intelligent enough to fill in this Census Form, I can surely make X on a ballot paper.' Suffragists claimed that tens of thousands took part. All-night activities were organised by groups of women so that they were absent from home at the time of the enumeration. Emmeline Pankhurst and her WSPU supporters gathered in Trafalgar Square at midnight on census night, and spent the remainder of the night at Aldwych skating rink. Similar 'parties' took place in Sheffield, Portsmouth and elsewhere. In Bath, the local organiser, Mildred Mansel, hired an empty house in Lansdowne Crescent; Mary Blathwayt was one of twenty-nine suffragettes to spend the night there, mainly sleeping on mattresses. Meanwhile, in South Wales, Emily Phipps and a group of friends evaded the census by spending the night in a cave on the Gower coast!

Emily Davison took the boldest step of all, concealing herself in the House of Commons itself from Saturday afternoon on 1 April until Monday afternoon (the census was to show where people were on the night of the Sunday, 2 April); however, she did not technically evade the census, as her presence there was duly noted by the Clerk of Works. Many women simply had their names left out of the household census returns, but it takes a great deal of local knowledge to find them. In Yarmouth, for example, Alice and Dorothy Turton, the wife and daughter of the vicar of Southtown, and Mrs George McLuckie, the wife of the Congregational minister, are conspicuous by their absence from the census returns for their homes; all three were members of the local suffrage group!

Other women added comments to their census returns. Some, like Mary Howey, simply added a slogan like 'VOTES FOR WOMEN'. Others made more coherent statements. Dorothea Rock wrote on hers that she would not fill the form in, as 'in the eyes of the Law women do not count, neither shall they be counted'. Dorothy Bowker played on the way that the form asked for information on deaf, dumb and blind people, writing, 'No Vote – No Census. I am Dumb politically. Blind to the Census. Deaf to Enumerators. Being classed with criminals, lunatics and paupers I prefer to give no further particulars.'

No arrests were made for failing to complete census forms; the only prosecutions arising out of census night were brought against a group of WSPU members who had spent the night on Wimbledon Common – and they were charged not with resisting the census but with damaging the grass by driving across it! Three vehicles had arrived at 1.45 a.m., with placards bearing the words, 'IF WE DON'T COUNT WE SHALL NOT BE COUNTED.' During the night, some women stood outside the vehicles, others sheltered inside them, the convoy leaving the common at about 7.30 in the morning. Katherine Willoughby Marshall was one of them. She recalled, 'Thousands of women all over the country never were counted that night, as we took empty houses and women slept on the floors while others were walking about the streets or stayed at our different headquarters, so that the census of women was a complete wash-out for government returns.' The vehicles were caravans driven by horses; the three drivers were eventually fined 2s each for driving on the turf. *The Times* took the Government line, describing the event as a failure, but Christabel Pankhurst said that it was a triumph – and that it had whetted their appetite for more!

On 5 May the 'second' Conciliation Bill passed its second reading by a majority of 167 and was referred to a Committee of the Whole House. This seemed like victory and the suffragettes were in celebratory mood. On 7 June, all the suffrage societies united – for the only time – in a procession of 40,000 supporters for the coronation of King George V. The suffragettes were sure that they had won, and the procession was a triumphant one. The marchers assembled on the Embankment, led once again by 'General' Drummond on her horse. Christabel Pankhurst described it as

the most joyous, beautiful and imposing of all our manifestations ... The other societies joined with us in our march through London, Mrs Fawcett at the head of her organisation, Mrs Despard at the head of hers, the many sectional suffrage societies, representing particular sections of women, such as the writers, the doctors, the actresses, the teachers and the rest. Women of all professions, trades and interests were there in their many thousands, women from every part of the kingdom and every part of the Empire, women from foreign lands. There was pageantry arranged by painters and sculptors. Queens and other great women of the past were represented, a hundred bands and countless flags and banners made the whole array beautiful to eye and ear. The processionists were so many that they marched five abreast. Mother walked at the head. Seven hundred women who had been prisoners for the vote had place of honour. The streets were thronged with cheering crowds. It was Suffrage Day! The climax of all peaceful effort! In this direction there was nothing more left to do.

Joan of Arc was again present on a white charger, on this occasion played by Joan Annan Bryce.

The march showed that most suffragettes were constitutionalists rather than militants, as *The Times* pointed out: 'The surprise of the demonstration, however, was the unexpected strength of the constitutionalists which it showed. The WSPU and the WFL combined were outnumbered and overshadowed by the NUWSS.'

Victory seemed within grasp, but the optimism turned to despair and anger later in the year. On 7 November, Asquith's announcement of a separate Manhood Suffrage Bill scuttled the suffragists' hopes for the Conciliation Bill. The truce was over – forever. A fortnight later, Mrs Pethick-Lawrence tried to lead a demonstration from Caxton Hall to the Commons, but was blocked by the police. More than 220 suffragettes were arrested during the demonstration and organised stone-throwing raid; about 150 were sent to prison for terms between one week and two months. For the WSPU, it was the beginning of all-out war.

Although the militants attracted all the publicity, the great majority of campaigners continued to be non-militants, working patiently within the law for the cause. Ray Strachey recalled how constitutionalist suffragists

> advocated the cause as they went about their ordinary lives. They lived as they had always lived, among people who knew and laughed at them, and they braved all the conventions by standing up at street corners and in the public parks to address passers-by. They chalked the pavements and sold their newspapers in the streets, they walked in the gutters with sandwich boards, and toiled from house to house canvassing for members, collecting money and advertising meetings.

Maude Royden was another dedicated to peaceful campaigning: 'For years I spoke to meetings every day in the week, often including Sunday, and sometimes twice in one day ... We all worked at this pitch and were all ready to help each other ... It is a grim business starting an open-air speech when there is no one present but your colleague and a dog. Of course the colleague takes her stand in front of you and assumes an air of passionate interest, but even that does not help greatly.'

Even the act of making a speech required great courage; it could easily lead to physical violence from male onlookers, especially if the women did not have men to protect them, as Hannah Mitchell's experiences some years earlier illustrate:

> We got all sorts of receptions. Once in Stockport about half a dozen of us were holding a meeting on the Armoury Square, when we were attacked by a crowd of roughs. Their conduct

was so terrifying that we fled for safety to the railway station, where the station officials shut all the gates when we were safely inside. Before our train left, someone handed in through the railings a bouquet of red roses.

One of the men with us on that occasion was Leonard Cox of the I.L.P., destined many years later to become Lord Mayor of Manchester. Leonard shared many of our worst experiences. One memorable night we had planned an outdoor meeting at Middleton. Either we had become too well known or the public had an uncanny gist of witch finding, for we were always recognised at once. As soon as I got off the tramcar, I heard shouts: 'Here's one of 'em.'

I was immediately surrounded by a gang of youths, who pushed and jostled me all the way to the Market Place. Here the local women were waiting by the two lorries intended for the platform. We managed to get together, but were not allowed to mount the lorries. That was the most menacing crowd I ever saw. Remembering it, I can visualize the sadism of the Nazi young men. We saw it there in the minds of the youths. They were encouraged by the inactivity of the police, who just stood round, some of them openly grinning and to whom we appealed in vain. These lads – there seemed to be hundreds of them – went to great lengths in their ill-treatment, especially of the younger women. I did not fare so badly, perhaps because I was better able to hide my fear. Standing there with my back to the lorry, I faced the crowd which hardly looked human, and cried out:

'We're not afraid of you.'

'We'll soon frighten you, missis,' they shouted.

'Never!' I said. 'You can kill us, but you can't frighten us.'

Leonard Cox, trying vainly to protect us, said I was so ghastly pale and spoke so firmly that the foremost hooligans fell back a few paces. But they wrecked our meeting, and chivvied us about so badly – the police were standing by! – that at last we took refuge in a shop whose owner invited us inside, threatening to drench with water any youth who dared to follow.

8

1912: The Argument of the Stone

On 16 February 1912, the women who had served three months for window-smashing in November were released. There was a celebratory meeting, at which Emmeline Pankhurst said, 'If the argument of the stone, that time-honoured official political argument is sufficient, then we will never use any stronger argument ... Why should women go to Parliament Square and be battered about and assaulted, and most important of all, produce less effect than when they throw stones?'

On Friday 1 March the window-breaking campaign began; Emmeline Pankhurst and Mabel Tuke, the honorary secretary of the WSPU, broke windows in Downing Street. At the same time, as reported in next day's *The Times*:

Some hundreds of women sallied forth carrying large muffs in which hammers were concealed, and at a given moment, according, it is believed, to a preconcerted signal, they went up to the plate-glass windows of various shops and deliberately smashed them with the hammers. The destruction done was immense. Along the Strand, in Cockspur Street, in the Haymarket, and Piccadilly, in Coventry Street, in Regent Street, in part of Oxford Street, and in Bond Street, many of the most conspicuous houses of business were attacked in this fashion. The large plate-glass windows of traders of all kinds – caterers, tobacconists, shoemakers, drapers, printsellers, stationers and many others – were ruined in this ruthless way. Were it not for the calculated and determined manner in which this work of devastation was carried out one would suppose it to have been wrought by demented and maniacal creatures; and even as it is a survey of the scene rather suggests that the mischief was done by people of unstable mental equilibrium.

The *Daily Mail* gave an impression of the occasion, as visual as was possible in an age before mobile phones to capture an event:

> From every part of the crowded and brilliantly lighted streets came the crash of splintered glass. People started as a window shattered at their side; suddenly there was another crash in front of them; on the other side of the street; behind everywhere ... Five minutes later the streets were a procession of excited groups, each surrounding a women wrecker being led in custody to the nearest police station.

It was followed up three days later, again as reported in *The Times*:

> Bands of zealots summoned from the country wandered about the West End of London, and, though apparently suffering from the nervousness of inexperience, did their best to emulate the window-breaking exploits of their

skilled London leaders on Friday night. The attacks began at eleven in the morning on the Brompton Road: three women, who were apparently studying the bill of fare outside the premises of the Aereated Bread Company, produced hammers and stones from their handbags and broke two large plate-glass windows. Three windows were broken at Harrods and eight at Harvey Nichols in Knightsbridge, and many in Kensington High Street. The windows of several Post Offices were broken, and in the evening a woman threw a stone through the window of Lord Cromer's house in Wimpole Street, while windows of Government offices in Whitehall and Parliament Square were attacked.

One of the window-breakers was Violet Aitken, the daughter of William Hay Aitken, a canon of Norwich Cathedral. His diary entry in March 1912 captures the horror he felt at Violet's activities:

A letter ... from Violet to the effect that she had been again arrested and this time for breaking plate glass windows. I am overwhelmed with shame and distress to think that a daughter of mine would do anything so wicked. I can only throw the whole matter on Him who is the great burden-bearer of his people. But my poor wife! It is heartbreaking to think of her being exposed in her old age to this horror.

A WSPU leaflet of the time addressed the anger of the shop owners:

You, a prosperous shopkeeper, have had your windows broken and your business interfered with, you are very angry about it, and no wonder. But you are angry with the wrong people. You are angry with the women who broke your windows, whereas you ought really to be angry with the people who drove them to it. Those people are the members of the present Government ... 'Well,' you may say, 'I sympathise with the women, but what have I got to do with it? Why should my windows be broken because Cabinet ministers are a band of rogues and tricksters?'

My dear Sir, you have got everything to do with it. You are a voter, and, therefore, the members of the Government are your servants, and if they do wrong, you are really responsible for it. That is why your windows have been broken – to make you realise your responsibility in the matter.

In fact, the spate of window-breaking, for example in March 1912 (which did £5,000 worth of damage), did not stop the advertisements in the suffragette newspapers, and even created a new group that profited – *The Times* of 14 June 1912 pointed out that insurance companies were reaping a huge harvest in profits.

Many of the women defended their actions in the court cases which followed. They had come from all over the country to answer their leader's call to action. Ethel Moorhead of Dundee said, 'I am a householder and a taxpayer without a vote. I came from Scotland at great personal inconvenience to myself to help my comrades.' Another Scottish stone-thrower was Alice Ker, one of the first women to qualify as a doctor, who had acted as unofficial doctor to hunger strikers in Walton Prison; her target was Harrods.

Eleanor Jacobs, the wife of the novelist W. W. Jacobs, had a hammer in her possession with a label reading, 'To Mr Lloyd George – a protest from a Welshwoman against repression.' *The Times* reported the following dialogue at her trial:

> Magistrate: What have you to say?
>
> Mrs Jacobs: I have done this because I think it is my duty as the mother of five children.
>
> Magistrate: What! Your duty as a mother of five children to smash property up!
>
> Mrs Jacobs: Yes, that is the only way we can protest against the action, or rather the inaction, of the Government in refusing justice.

Other window-breakers were old hands in the struggle, such as Sarah Carwin, who broke twelve windows in Regent Street. Others included Lettice Floyd, a full-time WSPU worker from 1908, together with her life-long partner Anne Williams, and Margaret Thompson, a teacher from Northumberland who broke windows in November 1911 and again in March 1912. She and her sister Mary had joined the NUWSS in 1904, moving to the WSPU by 1909. Another window-breaker was Hilda Brackenbury, the widow of a general, whose daughters have already been mentioned; she joined the WSPU in 1907 when she was seventy-five, and was in her eightieth year when she was arrested in March 1912 for smashing two windows in Whitehall.

On 6 March, the Pethick-Lawrences, Emmeline Pankhurst and Mabel Tuke were charged with conspiracy. Christabel Pankhurst was included but had not been caught. A description of her was circulated by the police: 'Wanted for conspiracy under the Malicious Damage to Property Act, Christabel Pankhurst, aged about 26; height about 5 ft 6 ins; fresh complexion, eyes dark, hair dark brown; usually wears a green tailor-made costume and a large fashionable hat.' In fact, she had already escaped to Paris.

The case against Mabel Tuke was dismissed because of her ill health. At the conspiracy trial, which began on 15 May, Emmeline Pankhurst made another poignant speech in which she explained how women had been driven to greater militancy by the stubborn opposition of the Government. The defendants were found guilty and, despite the jury's recommendation of leniency, were sentenced to nine months' imprisonment; in addition, Emmeline Pankhurst and Frederick Pethick-Lawrence were ordered to pay the prosecution costs. The Pethick-Lawrences and Emmeline threatened to go on hunger strike unless they were treated as political offenders and placed in the first division, a request that was granted. However, since the same privilege was not extended to other suffrage prisoners, all three joined with other imprisoned suffragists in a mass hunger strike that began on 19 June. Three days later, forcible feeding began. Holloway became a place of 'horror and torment', recollected Emmeline as she listened to the cries of women undergoing instrumental invasion of the body. When her own cell door was opened, she picked up a heavy earthenware jug and, with an air of authority, cried to the doctors and wardresses, 'If any of you dares so much as to take one step inside this cell I shall defend myself.' They all retreated. Emily Wilding Davison twice threw herself over the prison staircase in protest. Twenty-four of the suffragettes were moved from Holloway to Winson Green in Birmingham; six of them, including Violet Aitken and Sarah Carwin, were released in late June, because 'all have been forcibly fed and are seriously ill'. Some were able to return to London, but others remained in nursing homes.

Sylvia drew attention to the sacrifice made at this time by a nurse, Ellen Pitfield:

An ill-paid midwife, she had sustained on 'Black Friday' a wound which remained open. Arrested during the struggle that day, she was next morning committed to prison for two months. Her wound never healed, cancer developed, and after two unsuccessful operations she was declared incurable. A friend who saw it told me that the gaping wound in her thigh was like that of a poor, neglected sheep. Knowing herself a dying woman, she now entered the General Post Office, almost deserted on Sunday, and set there light to a basket of wood shavings she had brought with her. Having done so, she ran outside, broke a window, and gave herself up to a policeman. The little blaze had already been extinguished by the watchman, who came out of his box when he heard the smashing of glass. For this symbolic pretence at arson, she was committed for trial, bail being refused. On March 19th she was sentenced to six months' imprisonment, though she had been carried to the Court from her bed in the prison hospital, and the prison doctor testified that she was now so ill she would never walk again. The Men's Political Union organised a petition for her release which was effected in May. Sympathisers subscribed to send her to a nursing home, where she died in August. She had been arrested five times, and was forcibly fed in 1909. She had said on her release then: 'There are only two things that matter to me in the world: principle and liberty. For these I will fight as long as there is life in my veins. *I am no longer an individual, I am an instrument.*'

There were further protests. On 18 July a hatchet was 'thrown' into Asquith's carriage on an official visit to Dublin and suffragettes tried to set fire to the Theatre Royal where he was due to speak. The hatchet had been thrown by Mary Leigh, and might seem to have contradicted the suffragette code that there should be no physical violence – it was alleged that John Redmond, the Irish politician who was in the carriage with Asquith, was hurt by it. Mary Leigh was insistent that this was anti-suffragette propaganda; the hatchet was a small one with the words 'VOTES FOR WOMEN' written on it. She had placed it in the carriage, not thrown it, and the action could not possibly have hurt anyone. The case against her on this was dropped, but she and the other women who had set fire to the theatre were sentenced to five years in prison; they went on hunger strike and were released within nine weeks.

In 1906, the *Daily Mail* had coined the word 'suffragette'. In 1912, the WSPU itself tried to coin a new word for those suffragettes prepared to commit acts outside the law – the 'Outragette':

A new kind of woman has been created by the present Government, and the sooner she disappears the better for law and order and national dignity. This new woman is the Outragette. She began simply as one asking that women should have votes. Later she became a Suffragette and then a Militant, and finally, exasperated by the pettifogging evasions which are possible under our so-called system of representative government, she became an Outragette, a window-smasher, a rioter, wrecker and incendiary.

The Outragettes are now a formidable, though small, section of the women's movement, and not the least element of their strength is that they have in Mrs Pankhurst a leader capable of heroism and martyrdom. No one who followed her trial the other day at the Central Court will ever forget the burning passion of her defence, the high resolution which she proclaimed, just as have all those men and women who in the past have fought and suffered for our liberties. No one can condone an organised attack on society, but dull would we be of mind if we could not thrill at the spectacle of a brave woman defying the whole force of government and law.

Mrs Pankhurst was never intended to be a law-breaker. Surely her qualities of devotion to the good of her fellow-women marked her out to be a law-maker. Yet the Government, led by men whose chief cleverness lies in evasion and their ability to play tricks with parliamentary procedure, have made Mrs Pankhurst a law-breaker, have called into existence this wild tumult of Outragettes, women only in name and form, so completely have they been transformed into furies.

The word never caught on, but is useful in demonstrating that the people committing 'outrages' were only a tiny group among those women campaigning for the right to vote.

After window-smashing by WSPU in late 1911 and early 1912, Fawcett wrote that a small number of suffragists had 'temporarily lost all faith in human honour, in human sense of justice, and are attempting to grasp by violence what should be yielded to the growing conviction that our demand is based on justice and common sense'. Others saw the action in a more positive light, looking at its long-term significance. Charlotte Carmichael Stopes wrote, 'The flinging of stones is a primeval sign, ... as old as the invention of windows. It is a message that someone stands without who has not been able to make himself heard by ordinary means.' She concluded, 'We of the law-abiding societies would rather gain our enfranchisement in a common and ordinary way, and so would the militants.' Lady Rhondda, the Welsh suffragette who, as Margaret Mackworth, had been sentenced to a month in prison for setting fire to a pillar box, thought that 'the suffragettes broke more than windows with their stones. They broke the crust and conventions of a whole era.'

Tensions were ratcheted up even further with the first attempt by a suffragette to burn down the house of a Cabinet minister. On 19 July, Helen Craggs and another woman were arrested in the grounds of Nuneham House, the home of Mr Harcourt, the Colonial Secretary; the other woman escaped. Charges were bought against Ethel Smyth as being the second woman, but she was discharged. Helen's case came before the Assizes. A policeman said he had caught her and another woman in the grounds at 12.50 a.m. Incriminating items were found – a basket with tapers and oil in it, a handbag with an electric lantern and a glass-cutter; later, a cloth-covered hammer was also found. The handbag also contained a letter, signed 'A Suffragette', presumably to be left on the scene. It read,

Sir, it is with a deep sense of my responsibility and with a sincere conviction that my action is justifiable that I have taken a serious step in the cause of women's enfranchisement.

I profoundly regret that the forty long years of peaceful agitation and petitioning on the part of women was of no avail to secure for them their enfranchisement, and still more do I deplore that though during the last six years the demand for political liberty for women has become the greatest agitation of the time, politicians were content to see its supporters violently treated and unjustly imprisoned rather than give them the long-delayed and much-needed measure of justice which they demanded. I myself have taken part in every peaceful method of propaganda and petition and many wiser than I have done the same, but I have been driven to realize that it has been of no avail, so now I have accepted the challenge given by Mr Hobhouse at Bristol, and I have done something drastic. When Cabinet ministers tell us that violence is the only argument they understand, it becomes our duty to give them the argument, therefore I have done my duty.

Women have a growing sense of proportion in this matter. They see around them the most appalling evils in the social order. They see children born into conditions which maim them physically and mentally for life. They see their fellow women working in the sweated industries at a wage which makes their life a living death, or sacrificed as white slaves to a life which is worse than death. I feel that I dare not acquiesce in such a state of things, and that delay on my part would be criminal. I have, therefore, done what I have done with a full sense of my responsibility, knowing that the only way to right these terrible wrongs is to put into women's hands the weapon of the Parliamentary vote. Men and women of the past have done violence and have suffered and died in order to put wrong things right, and to win freedom for themselves and others. I am not ashamed – rather I am proud – that in my way I, too, have followed this proud tradition.

Finally it rests with the present Government to decide how much destruction, how great the violence, to which women like myself will be reluctantly driven before our most just demand is granted.

Helen was sentenced to nine months in prison, with hard labour. Hobhouse had made a speech in Bristol in which he said that he had not seen a 'popular sentimental uprising' in favour of women's suffrage as there had been in the campaign for the vote for men, citing the way Nottingham Castle had been burnt down by protesters in 1832.

In October there was a further split in the WSPU ranks, with the Pethick-Lawrences breaking with the Pankhursts over the amount of violence that had come into the campaign. The Pethick-Lawrences kept control of their paper, *Votes For Women*, so the WSPU started a new one, *The Suffragette*, which was edited by Cicely Hale; it did not have the great sales of its rival, but sold a very respectable 17,000 a week at its height. *The Suffragette* urged women to join the WSPU:

> Do not flatter yourself that you are impartial: you cannot be that. If you acquiesce you strengthen the hands of the Government in its trickery and brutality, and consequently delay the vote. If you are not with the cause of Freedom, you are against it.

Alongside the dramatic episodes, the great majority of women campaigners were going on as before, organising meetings at a local level and campaigning in by-elections. The NUWSS supported whichever candidate would pledge himself to support suffrage for women, but the WSPU, because their aim was the fall of the Liberal Government, urged support for whichever candidate was most likely to defeat the Liberal. This could result in a paradox, as in the North West Norfolk by-election in May 1912. There were two candidates, a Liberal, Edward Hemmerde, and a Conservative, Philip Jodrell. Jodrell was against giving women the vote, Hemmerde was in favour. The NUWSS naturally supported Hemmerde, but the WSPU's policy of opposing all Liberals drove it to support Jodrell – even though he was opposed to women's suffrage!

Later in the year, a by-election was fought specifically on the issue of women's suffrage. On 11 November 1912 George Lansbury, Labour MP for Bromley and Bow in East London, announced that he would resign his seat and fight in the subsequent by-election on the single issue of votes for women. The poll was to be on 26 November. Suffragists, suffragettes and their opponents flocked to the area. Lansbury's only opponent was Reginald Blair, a Unionist and an opponent of votes for women, which simplified the issues. Lansbury was popular with the working-class women of the constituency, but of course they did not have the vote. The predominantly upper- and middle-class suffragettes appear to have alienated the working men who did have the vote. In the end, Lansbury was defeated by 751 votes. He continued to support women's suffrage and was one of the few men to participate in a hunger strike after being arrested in April 1913; he was quickly released.

The Suffragette urged its supporters to take action: 'Women will never get the vote except by creating an intolerable situation for all the selfish and apathetic people who stand in their way.' In this spirit, suffragettes were constantly thinking of new ways in which to protest. The defeat at Bromley and Bow was followed by a national campaign of attacks on pillar boxes that lasted for five weeks; as well as burning rags, chemicals were poured into the boxes. Emily Davison is said to have been the first to set fire to a pillar box, attacking the one in Parliament Street post office in November 1911: she was sentenced to six months in prison. By December 1912, over 5,000 letters in post boxes had been damaged; the Post Office claimed that it had failed to deliver just thirteen letters and seven postcards due to their state, but this figure was naturally disputed by the suffragettes. To drop a flaming rag or acid into a post box was a daunting enough task for many a respectable woman, who had to nerve themselves to the task. One,

Maud Kate Smith, later recalled, 'It made me so ill because I hated doing it … but if it's your job, it's your job, you see. I never turned back.' Jessie Stephen, a domestic servant in Glasgow, had no such qualms; she 'walked from my place of service in my uniform and dropped the acid container in the pillar-box and made my way back without interruption by anyone. A few minutes later the contents were aflame.' It was a typical stunt, causing inconvenience but no possible harm to anyone, except perhaps the suffragette herself; one of the few arrests was of a Liverpool University student who had both hands badly burnt by a preparation containing phosphorous. Sylvia Pankhurst recalled later that one of the Holloway officers, who had been stationed in Walton Gaol at the time, told her long afterwards, 'It was terrible to see how the poor mortal had been burned!'

Another easy 'hit' was to make a false fire call from a public telephone; this was done 176 times in 1911, 425 in 1912 and still more frequently in 1913. In December 1912, Elsie Howey was gaoled for two months for giving a false fire alarm, an incident which illustrated her personal popularity; seventy-five 'working men and farmers' from Malvern wrote to their MP demanding a reduced punishment for their 'much loved' local suffragette.

The Suffragette claimed that there were 150 serious attacks on property in 1912, and the increasing pace of the campaign meant more prison sentences; 240 women were sent to prison for suffragette 'outrages' in 1912, compared with 188 in 1911 and 116 in 1910.

9
1913: Guerilla Warfare, a Death and a Pilgrimage

There was yet another split within the ranks of the WSPU. Sylvia Pankhurst had long been working with the poor in the East End of London, and the empowering of women had become more important to her than the single issue of the franchise; Sylvia, unlike her mother Emmeline and sister Christabel, came to hold the view that the vote was not everything. As a result, she and the East London Federation of Suffragettes broke off from the WSPU. Her supporters in the East End of London included Jessie Stephen, who had taken part in the pillar box campaign in Glasgow, and Zelie Emerson, who was forcibly fed with Sylvia after a window-breaking attack.

On 23 January, a deputation of twenty working women, selected from a group of 300 and headed by Mrs Drummond and Annie Kenny of the WSPU, were received at the Treasury by Lloyd George, the Chancellor of the Exchequer. They came from fifteen British cities and represented the wide range of occupations in which women were employed: schoolteachers (including Miss Bonnett, a London headmistress), shop assistants, machinists, factory workers, laundry women from the East End of London, workers in the boot and shoe trade in Leicester, weavers and other textile workers in Lancashire and Yorkshire (including Mrs Ashworth of Rossendale and Mrs Norton, a Yorkshire weaver), hospital nurses in uniform, a colliery worker and Scottish fisherwomen. One of the textile workers was Leonora Cohen from Leeds, who told Lloyd George that women in the industry worked for 3½d an hour, while men were paid 6½d for exactly the same work. The colliery worker was Miss Morgan, who wore her working clothes and clogs. Although the politicians could not know it, she was a local hero; she helped take care of the dying in the Hulton Colliery disaster of December 1910, in which 344 miners had been killed.

However, on the same day as this meeting, the Speaker announced that he had decided it was not possible to add clauses allowing women's franchise to the Franchise Bill currently being considered in Parliament; a totally new Bill would have to be drawn up. In practice this meant that would be no women's suffrage in the immediate future. This meant war. Mrs Pankhurst declared, 'We will fight for the vote as Garibaldi fought for Italian freedom.' At a meeting held at this time, she said, 'It is guerilla warfare that we declare this afternoon,' and announced that only human life would be sacred. At once, windows of Government offices were smashed; thirty women were arrested.

In February, a new target was found: golf courses. This was again a clever choice – most golf courses only allowed men to play on them – even in the twenty-first century, the rights of women are very restricted on some courses. It was also difficult to keep out determined women; turf on greens was cut with sharp tools, slogans such as 'NO VOTES, NO

GOLF' and 'BETTER BE HOSTILE THAN INDIFFERENT' emblazoned, hole flags replaced with suffragette ones. Other targets included telephone wires and yet more pillar boxes. In Monmouthshire a railway signal wire was cut; all the 'outrages' were accompanied by slogans of 'Votes for Women'.

At a series of meetings, Emmeline Pankhurst openly encouraged a policy of stronger militancy and her followers were quick to respond. The arson campaign now got underway in earnest. On 12 February, the suffragettes burned down a refreshment kiosk in Regent's Park. Several empty petrol cans were found nearby, and the words VOTES FOR WOMEN had been scratched into the gravel path. The damage was estimated at between £600 and £700. This was the first incident in a programme of damage to empty buildings. On 19 February, a new house being built for Lloyd George near Walton Heath Golf Course, Walton-on-the-Hill, Surrey, was blown up. A loud explosion occurred at 6.10 a.m., waking people in nearby houses and rattling the windows of an inn 300 yards away. A dozen workmen were due to start their shift at 6.30 a.m.; they found that the servants' wing of the house had been wrecked in the explosion. A second 'bomb' in the main stairway had not gone off:

> In the cupboard stood a small, square, tightly-corded tin, containing black powder. The slide of the canister had been opened, and two fuses, consisting of rag soaked in paraffin, had been inserted in the aperture. These fuses trailed along the floor for some distance to a heap of shavings, also saturated

in paraffin, and set up in the midst of these was a candle. The wick of the candle had been lighted, but three inches of tallow still remained when the searchers found it. It had been extinguished before then, possibly by the force of the explosion of the similar machine in the servants' wing, but more probably by the exclusion of air from the cupboard.

There was, of course, no suggestion that Emmeline Pankhurst had set the bomb herself, but she was happy to take overall responsibility for the work of one of her 'soldiers'. The day after the Walton explosion, she said, 'I have advised, I have incited, I have conspired; and the authorities need not look for the women who have done what they did last night, because I myself accept full responsibility for it.' At Chelsea Town Hall on 21 February she taunted the authorities:

The police were searching for the perpetrators of the outrage. They had found a golosh [overshoe] and two hatpins without heads and were still searching, while she, who had accepted full responsibility several times, was still at large. Why had they not taken her? She supposed the authorities thought it would be more difficult to manage things with her in Holloway than with her outside. At any rate, she did not delude herself into thinking it was out of any consideration for herself. It was very wrong that other women should be sent to prison while she, who had incited them to do the things, should be out of prison. When the public got the right point of view of what had been done by the women it would be realized that the women's insurrection was characterized by a very much larger amount of self-restraint than men's insurrections. The methods they had adopted did not involve the sacrifice of any human lives. They were humane, because they were directed only against property, which could be built up again when the women's war was ended. But, short of sacrificing human life, women meant to do everything that became necessary to settle the political status of women.

Emmeline Pankhurst was arrested on 24 February and accepted full responsibility; on 3 April she was sentenced at the Old Bailey to three years' penal servitude for the damage to Lloyd George's house. Between her arrest and her trial, the Government introduced its new weapon. More suffragettes in prison meant more hunger strikes and more forced feeding. There was a public outcry against this and many MPs were also opposed, some preferring the alternative – that the women should be allowed to die. Reginald McKenna disagreed, as he did not want to create martyrs for the cause; besides, he had what a later generation would call a 'cunning plan'.

The Prisoners' Temporary Discharge for Ill Health Bill was introduced into Parliament on 25 March and became law in April. Under the Act, a hunger striker would be released if her life was in danger but would have to go back to prison as soon as she was well enough to do so. At the committee stage, McKenna said,

All I am dealing with now is a Bill to enable me to release a prisoner from prison without giving an absolute remission of the sentence. I want to keep the sentence alive. If I have to release a prisoner upon her own misconduct, I do not think she should have unconditional release or a remission of the sentence, and I ask for such powers as will enable me, as far as I can, to compel the service of the remainder of the sentence.

Keir Hardie moved an amendment that the Bill should not apply to any female prisoner who had been force fed. He looked at a specific case, Zelie Emerson, who had carried on a daily warfare against being force-fed until liberated when her sentence of two months was almost expired. Under the proposed Act, she would be nursed and doctored until she 'was in a condition to go back to once more fight the wardresses and the doctors she is taken back. Can anything more inhuman and more barbarous be conceived?' However, the Bill was passed by 294 votes to 56. Fred Pethick-Lawrence dubbed it 'the Cat and Mouse Act', and it has come down to history under this name. From this date, there was a continual cycle of events in the lives of the leading suffragettes: arrest, followed by hunger strike in prison, which led to release under licence. When sufficiently recovered, the suffragette would then try to hold meetings or engage in other activities and eventually would be caught by the authorities and sent to prison, where she would again go on hunger strike. Most of the London suffragettes went to the 'safe house' of the Brackenbury family home in Campden Hill Square to recover; it became known as 'Mouse Castle'. Police were stationed outside, but the 'mice' often managed to escape.

The increased violence aroused the hostility of many; there were 10,000 people at one suffragette meeting at Hyde

Park but many were opponents of female suffrage. Flora Drummond was shouted down when she tried to speak and clods of earth were thrown at her and the other speakers, followed by pebbles, wads of paper and oranges. There were similar disturbances at a meeting on Wimbledon Common on the same day, where the crowd was estimated at 8,000 or 9,000.

Militant suffragettes were active throughout the country, far too many to be set down. A typical individual 'outrage' was one in Cambridge on 18 May; two buildings were burned down in the town, first a new house being built for a Mrs Spencer of Castle Street, then a new genetics laboratory. Suffragette leaflets were found in both. A lady's gold watch was discovered outside the window of the laboratory which had been used to get in. On 22 May a twenty-two-year-old Norwich schoolteacher, Miriam Pratt, was arrested; she had been 'shopped' by her uncle, a policeman, who had recognised the watch. Blood had been found where the arsonist had cut herself while scraping out the putty around the window; Miriam had a corresponding wound. She was bailed and took part in suffragette meetings over the summer. On 14 October, her trial was held at last. In fact the arson attempt had been put together by Olive Bartels, the WSPU organiser in Cambridge, who had chosen the target and bought and supplied the paraffin used, but there is no doubt that it was Miriam Pratt who did the actual deed. She was sentenced to eighteen months in prison; naturally, she was also dismissed from her teaching post. Miriam immediately went on hunger strike and was transferred to Holloway. She was very soon released for seven days under the Cat and Mouse Act, and went to recover with friends in Kensington.

Other houses were burnt down as the arson attacks grew more common – but, it must be stressed, they were always houses that were unoccupied; no life, apart from that of the perpetrator, was put at risk. On 20 March, for example, a house at Egham owned by Lady White was destroyed; it had been used as a country house by her late husband. Many of the arsonists were not caught but some were, and some took pride in publicising what they had done. Edith Rigby of Preston came before the courts charged with an attack on Liverpool Cotton Exchange. She justified this by saying that Lancashire cotton merchants had made themselves wealthy by exploiting female labour – and the women had no vote! She went on to announce that she was the otherwise unknown 'arsonist' who had burnt down the bungalow at Rivington Pike belonging to Sir William Lever.

The more dramatic the stunt, the more publicity it would gather. In February, a woman went into the Jewel House in the Tower of London. She took out an iron bar that she had concealed underneath her coat and threw it at a glass showcase that contained the insignia of the Orders of Merit. Wrapped around the bar was a paper, which read, 'This is my protest against the Government's treachery to the working women of Great Britain.' The assailant was Leonora Cohen; she had come down from her home town of Leeds to be part of the deputation to Lloyd George, and had decided to stay on in London to make the attack. She was arrested by the Tower's beefeaters and charged with causing malicious damage; however, it was decided in court that the damage was below the legal limit of £5 and she was acquitted by the jury. In an interview later in life, she explained why she had acted: 'Life was hard. My mother would say, "Leonora, if only we women had a say in things," but we hadn't. A drunken lout of a man opposite had a vote simply because he was a male. I vowed I'd try to change things.'

Death at the Derby, 4 June 1913

Perhaps the most sensational single event in the suffragette campaign occurred on 4 June 1913. Emily Davison bought a third-class return ticket to Epsom, and stood at Tattenham Corner to watch the Derby. As the king's horse, Anmer, approached, she ran onto the course and grabbed its bridle. The horse rolled over her, injuring her severely. She lingered in hospital for several days, her bed becoming a shrine, the WSPU badge at its head and their colours on the screen around it. She died at 4.30 p.m. on 8 June. It is not clear if she had deliberately chosen to die, but she clearly accepted the risk and she became the movement's first publicly acclaimed martyr. Her death naturally filled the newspapers for days, giving enormous publicity to the cause. The funeral followed on 14 June. Her coffin was carried across London at the head of an enormous procession of women to St George's Bloomsbury, where the service was held. Elsie Howey rode beside the coffin, once again dressed as Joan of Arc. The procession then continued to King's Cross station, where the coffin was put onto a train to Morpeth, Emily's home town, for burial.

Millicent Fawcett acknowledged Emily as a martyr for the cause: 'She had deliberately sacrificed her life in order, in this sensational way, to draw the attention of the whole world to the determination of women to share in the heritage of freedom which was the boast of every man in the country ... She had died for her cause ... Emily Davison had shown that she knew how to die.' Self-sacrifice was a major theme at this time, and Emily may have drawn her inspiration from male examples such as the men on the *Titanic* who put women and children first in April 1912, and the heroism of Captain Scott and his comrades whose deaths in March 1912 only became known a year later. Emily had shown women could also make the supreme sacrifice in a worthwhile cause.

There was an immediate response by Emily Davison's supporters. On the night of her death the greater part of the grandstand at Hurst Park was destroyed by fire. Many years later, Kitty Marion, the perpetrator, recalled how it was done. She and Clara Giveen went to have a look at the racecourse, and saw that the only way in was over a high fence with spikes and barbed wire on top. They borrowed a piece of carpet from Kitty's landlady, and packed a suitcase with their equipment. They set out at 9 p.m. on the Sunday night, travelling by train and then by tram to the bridge near Hampton Court Palace. They managed to climb the fence with the aid of a tool shed which was next to it – and their piece of carpet! Once inside, they found an unlocked door into the grandstand and there spread their inflammable material. As a timer they placed a candle on the material and lit it. They thought it would take at least an hour to burn down and start the fire so they would have time to get well away. However, probably the candle fell over; as they were climbing back over the fence the grandstand was already well ablaze. They walked over the bridge and through Richmond and Kew, once asking a policeman to direct them. When he asked why they were out so late – it was now well after 1.00 a.m. – Kitty told him that she was a music-hall singer on her way home. The next morning the two women were arrested. They were both given long prison sentences but went on hunger strike in prison and were eventually released under the Cat and Mouse Act; Kitty Marion had been force-fed an incredible 232 times. Racecourse stands became a favourite target of suffragette attack; not only were they certain to be empty if attacked at night, but the memory of Emily Davison was always there.

Both suffrage leaders dealt with the situation with a kind of gallows humour. Emmeline Pankhurst said that Emily 'gave up her life for the woman's cause by throwing herself in the path of the thing, next to property, held most sacred to Englishmen – sport'. Millicent Fawcett made a comparison of gender; after the incident, the king asked about the jockey, the queen about the injured woman! In fact, it was Queen Mary who asked first about the jockey – and who referred to Emily Davison as 'that horrid woman'.

Emmeline Pankhurst, on release under the Cat and Mouse Act, had tried to attend Emily Davison's funeral, but had been re-arrested on leaving her home. Sent back to prison, she adopted a new weapon, terrible to those who used it, the thirst strike:

The hunger strike I have described as a terrible ordeal, but it is a mild experience compared with the thirst strike, which is from beginning to end simple unmitigated torture.

Hunger striking reduces a person's weight very quickly, but thirst striking reduces weight so alarmingly fast that prison doctors were at first thrown into absolute panic of fright. Later they became somewhat hardened, but even now they regard the thirst strike with terror. I am not sure that I can convey to the reader the effect of days spent without a single drop of water taken into the system. The body cannot endure loss of moisture. It cries out in protest with every nerve. The muscles waste, the skin becomes shrunken and flabby, the facial appearance alters horribly, all these outward symptoms being eloquent suffering of the entire physical being. Every natural function is, of course, suspended, and the poisons which are unable to pass out of the body are retained and absorbed. The body becomes cold and shivery, there is constant headache and nausea, and sometimes there is fever. The mouth and tongue become coated and swollen, the throat thickens and the voice sinks to a thready whisper.

Emmeline was released after three days, but never completely recovered from the jaundice that she suffered because of her thirst strike.

The WSPU activities naturally dominated the newspapers, as they were designed to do, but far more women expressed their outrage in the form of peaceful protest, holding public meetings and going on protest marches. The culmination of this was the great 'Pilgrimage'. The marchers deliberately wore plain clothing – blouses, skirts and coats of white, grey, black or navy. This made the cockades on their hats and their haversacks in NUWSS colours stand out all the more.

As Millicent Fawcett wrote,

Eight routes were selected – the great North Road, the Fen Country, the East Coast Road, Watling Street, the West Country Road, the Portsmouth Road, the Brighton road, and the Kentish Pilgrims' Way. The Pilgrims journeyed on foot with occasional lifts, friends lending motors for luggage and the less robust of the Pilgrims. The whole thing caught on to an enormous extent; villagers ran out to meet us, begging us to stop and give us a meeting; all kinds of hospitality were offered and greatly accepted. When once people understood that we had no desire to hurt anybody nor to damage anything, they gave us a most cordial reception.

She acknowledged that in some towns, the reception was not so friendly, blaming this on the unpopularity of the militants: 'Hooligans sometimes declined to believe that we were non-militant, and demonstrated their enthusiasm for law and order by throwing dead rats, potatoes, rotten eggs, and other garbage at our speakers. No real harm was done to any of us, but occasionally the services of the police were needed to protect our speakers.' The ladies from Cornwall passed through Devon on their way, holding a meeting at Newton Abbot; in a sharp difference in attitude compared with the by-election of a few years earlier, this time there was a crowd of 3,000 to listen – and no disturbance whatsoever.

The Pilgrimage culminated in a huge meeting at Hyde Park on 26 July, with nineteen platforms representing the nineteen federations of the NUWSS, which had spent £35 on advertisements on sixty London buses and on the tubes. The investment more than paid for itself; the meeting attracted about 70,000 people and was a huge propaganda success. It has been said that it helped dispel the ill will created by militant activity and once more portray the suffragette movement in a favourable light.

Sylvia Pankhurst was dismissive: 'On Saturday July 26th, the Suffrage 'Pilgrims' organised by the NUWSS held a mass meeting in Hyde Park. For weeks they had been marching towards London, from north, south, east and west, holding meetings by the way ... The NUWSS never captured the interest of the multitude. It was so staid, so willing to wait, so incorrigibly leisurely.' However, the NUWSS was working in very practical ways; its Election Fighting Fund supplied financial help to candidates in elections who favoured women's suffrage, in practice Labour Party candidates, and they began to reach out more into the working class, with organisers such as Ada Nield Chew and Selina Cooper. The NUWSS also worked on getting pro-suffrage resolutions from trade unions; some 342 trade unions as well as trades councils and ILP branches were represented at a suffrage rally in the Albert Hall in February 1914.

Contrasts in attitudes among suffragettes can be seen in the different role models that they adopted. Elsie Howey achieved national recognition when she headed WSPU demonstrations through London dressed as Joan of Arc, in a full set of armour, 'astride a great white charger'. Christabel Pankhurst described Joan of Arc as the 'patron saint' of the suffragette movement – godly, resolute and militant, but also a passive martyr. Mary Richardson, when on hunger strike, wrote to Kitty Marion, 'I have been thinking of Joan of Arc today – How marvellous she was all alone, with vile men night and day so tormented.' Millicent Fawcett also spoke of 'the special wonder of Joan', her 'union of the man and of the woman, strength and tenderness'. However, the Women's Freedom League preferred to take Florence Nightingale as their role model, stressing her self-sacrifice, her skills as an administrator and her work to improve the conditions in which people lived; many suffragettes were medical workers or teachers. Other parts of the country might find inspiration in their own past; in 1912, Ethel Moorhead damaged the great monument to William Wallace in Stirling (we have already seen the part played in the struggle by one of his descendants). Her motive was to draw the parallel between Scotland's fight for liberty and that of the suffragettes. Ethel was sent to Perth Prison, where she became the first Scottish suffragette to be force-fed.

10
1914 and Afterwards

The *Rokeby Venus*

Another weapon in the armoury of the militant suffragette was the attempted destruction of works of art, which reached its climax in the spring of 1914, but had begun a year earlier, when Annie Kenney had said that the militants wanted 'to see the British Museum and the National Gallery closed and all the shops barricaded'. On 10 March, Mary Richardson went into the National Gallery and slashed the *Rokeby Venus*, the Velazquez painting, as a protest against the arrest of Emmeline Pankhurst in Glasgow on the previous day. Her motive was not merely the destruction of a work of art; just as Venus was 'the most beautiful woman in mythological history', it was right that a symbolic protest should be made against what the Government was doing to Mrs Pankhurst, 'the most beautiful character in modern history'. In later life, she also said that she hated women being 'used' as nudes and had seen the painting gloated over by men. She was sentenced to six months in prison, forcibly fed but soon released. She was rearrested and released several times under the Cat and Mouse Act; according to a doctor's report, her mouth was scarred from the fingernails of prison officials. Other women damaged works of art without advancing such justifications, such as Gertrude Ansell and Mary Spencer, who damaged paintings at the Royal Academy, and Freda Graham who damaged pictures at the National Gallery. All three were sent to prison, where they went on hunger strike.

The pitch that suffragette activities had now reached can be seen by looking at incidents in just one typical area, that of East Anglia – not an area normally associated with such action. In April 1914, the National Union of Teachers held their annual conference at Lowestoft. Suffragettes, both militant and non-militant, were there of course; there was a large crowd on the Esplanade on Sunday 5 April to hear militant speakers. On the following Sunday a service was held at St John's church to welcome the teachers, led by the Bishop of Norwich. The service was interrupted many times by women shouting slogans in support of Mrs Pankhurst, and urging the bishop to help stop the forcible feeding of women. The bishop read a prepared sermon welcoming the teachers and making no comment about the actions of the suffragettes. The suffragettes later justified their action. They said that, when Mrs Pankhurst was in prison in Exeter, the Bishop of Exeter had promised to say a prayer for her and other militants on hunger strike. They were asking the Bishop of Norwich to do the same. They also commented on the 'excessive violence' used to eject them from the church.

The non-militant suffragettes held a meeting at the Marina Theatre on 14 April. The speakers included Millicent Fawcett. The WSPU held a meeting at the Hippodrome. Mrs Pankhurst was going to appear but was too ill to attend; she had not recovered from the violent way in which she was treated by the police when they had arrested her in Glasgow five weeks earlier. Two other top names in the WSPU, Flora Drummond and Annie Kenney, did speak. For Annie this was a great risk – she was wanted by the police under the Cat and Mouse Act. She later recalled what had happened:

Mrs Pankhurst had been asked to speak, but she was too ill, so I volunteered. I shall never forget my flight from 'Mouse Castle'.

At the bottom of Campden Hill the detectives were in full force night and day. And at the top were men we looked on with suspicion. What was I to do? How could I escape? We found that we had members in a house whose side-garden wall was the back-garden wall of 'Mouse Castle'. That was the way of exit: no other way was possible. The people were approached and they consented for rope ladders to be used, and all other necessaries for me to get away.

My 'get-up' was amusing: a black bathing-costume, black stocking on the arms as well as legs, a black veil with holes for me to see where I was going. I looked just like the Black Cat of the pantomime.

She was sheltered at a vicarage a few miles from Lowestoft and went to the meeting dressed as a respectable aunt, with a fur, glasses and shoes without high heels, 'which made me look small'. She was accompanied by another suffragette dressed as her schoolgirl niece. Annie changed and spoke, making an emotive speech:

The only way you can stop militant methods is by giving women the vote and the sooner you learn the lesson the better. We shall go on, and on, and on, and go to prison and come out of prison and be as bad as ever ... They thought they would crush us if they put us in prison. When you are on hunger strike and thirst strike, your suffering is very great; your tongue is swollen, your lips are swollen and your mouth is swollen. The whole body twitches and you have unendurable sensations. But you have no fear at all, though you know perfectly well you may never leave prison alive. There is something in this movement that no power of opposition whether of the Government or the people can stop.

Her recollections continue: 'The meeting went wild with enthusiasm. Before it was over I changed my dress, and I marched out as a girl with my hair hanging loosely down, a picture-hat on my head, a scarf round with my neck and my eyebrows blackened, and my lips and cheeks a little rouged. I got safely away and safely back in London, for which I felt happy. I was once again in the thick of the fight.' A crowd tried to rush the building after the meeting: Mrs Drummond was still in the building and, apparently, was smuggled out disguised as a man.

On 17 April, the pavilion on the Britannia Pier in Yarmouth was destroyed by fire. According to *The Suffragette*, which carried a photograph of the blazing building, suffragette messages were found on the beach nearby:

VOTES FOR WOMEN. MR McKENNA HAS NEARLY KILLED MRS PANKHURST. WE CAN SHOW NO MERCY UNTIL WOMEN ARE ENFRANCHISED.

Some days later, it was Felixstowe that received the suffragette attack. In the words of a letter from East Suffolk police to the Home Secretary,

Shortly after 4.15 on the morning of 28th April the Bath Hotel at Felixstowe in this county was found to be on fire and as a result became totally destroyed, the brickwork alone being left standing, the damage being estimated at £30,000. The premises were unoccupied and in the hands of the decorators.

On the previous Friday, 24th April, stacks value £350, the property of Mr E. G. Prettyman MP, and on Sunday 26th April a stack value £450 the property of Mr Spencer Dawson, were fired at Bucklesham and Stratton Hall respectively.

In all the cases papers were left indicating that the fires were caused by Suffragettes, and in the two cases mentioned in the second paragraph two women on bicycles were seen in the vicinity of the stacks before they were found to be on fire.

In these circumstances, after the Bath hotel fire, the police directed their energies to finding two women at Felixstowe who were absent from their lodgings on the night of the 28th April and as a result it was found that the two women now in custody told their landlady that they were going to Ipswich for the night and would return to their rooms the next morning. Subsequent enquiries elicited that these two women were in occupation of a so called beach tent, a wooden structure like a cycle house, there are a number of these at Felixstowe hired by visitors. This hut is quite near the Bath Hotel and two women were seen there at 10 p.m. on the night before the fire.

The two women were arrested about 1.30 p.m. on the 28th and with their belongings were found a hammer, a glazier's diamond, a pair of pincers, and a bottle containing lump phosphorous in water.

An entrance was made into the hotel by cutting out part of a pane of glass which had previously smeared with soft soap and covered with wadding. A tin containing soft soap was found in the hut occupied by these women.

They refused their names and to account for their whereabouts on the night of the 28th.

The women were Hilda Byron and Florence Tunks. A coded diary by Hilda was found, which suggested that not only were the pair in Yarmouth at the time of the Britannia Pier fire, but that other entries might match up with arson attacks in the first four months of 1914 in Scotland, Somerset, Birmingham and Belfast; they appear to have been busy in the suffragette cause. However, they were charged only with the Felixstowe fire.

Although women like these and Annie Kenney clearly enjoyed the excitement of illegal activity, they were still very much in the minority among suffragists and suffragettes. Most were respectable women who dreaded breaking the law, having to nerve themselves for the task. Hazel Inglis recalled that the ten minutes before smashing a window were the worst; 'that's the awful time'. Amber Bianco-White had armed herself to smash a window, but, when the moment came, simply could not bring herself to do it: 'The contents of the window did not seem to matter, but look at that lovely glass.' Pleasance Pendred, a London schoolteacher arrested for damaging property in 1913, told the court, 'You little know how we women have to screw up and screw up our courage to acting point.' When Leonora Cohen decided to make her assault at the Tower of London, she was so nervous that she did not get off the Underground when she reached the stop; she travelled all the way around the Circle Line before nerving herself for her task. Their reluctance to be revolutionaries was shown in some very English compromises, at least at the beginning of the window-smashing campaign; those throwing them often wrapped them in paper first to minimise the chance of anyone being hurt. This was also the opportunity to send a written message with the stone. Others had their stone on a string to keep some control of where it went!

There was another huge – and well-publicised – demonstration in London on 21 May. Mrs Pankhurst and her supporters tried to present a petition to the king at Buckingham Palace. The police were ready and formed a cordon; just one woman got through it and she was unable to reach the palace gates. There were sixty-seven arrests. Once again, the protesters thought they had been met with unnecessary force. Eleanor Higginson of Preston recalled that 'they mauled us about the shoulders and we were all black and blue the next day'.

Churches were not immune. In March, one or more women hid in Birmingham Cathedral during the day, opening up the doors at night to let in others; they proceeded to daub almost the whole of the interior of the building with suffrage slogans in white paint – 'VOTES FOR WOMEN'; 'STOP

FORCIBLE FEEDING' and others. On 11 June, a small bomb went off in Westminster Abbey, slightly damaging the Coronation Chair.

Two scenes in London courts on 13 July 1914 showed how farcical proceedings had become. At Westminster Police Court, Annie Bell was charged with placing a bomb in the church of St John the Evangelist, Smith Square. She had attended evensong and at the end of the service was seen to bend forward in one of the pews with a light in her hand. The police were sent for and a bomb was found, a tin canister filled with gunpowder, with a candle as a fuse. Annie Bell was out from Holloway under the Cat and Mouse Act. Alice Oakley, one of the church workers, gave evidence that she saw Bell lighting the candle. Bell responded, 'I should like to congratulate witness on her smartness. I think it is worthy of a better cause. I think she would make a good suffragette, and I should advise her to join the cause. I set off the bomb right enough. I meant it to go off and blow up the church.' Later, she said, 'I am proud of having done it. The only thing that I am sorry for is that the beastly thing would not go off.' She then 'stretched herself at full length on the seat at the back of the dock and asked that someone should wake her up when the case was over. She also asked for a pillow. She did not go to sleep, however, but continued to talk to the Court. On being remanded for a week, she remarked to the magistrate as she left the Court, "Goodbye, old bully."'

At Bow Street Court on the same day, five women from the Women's Freedom League also showed their contempt for the legal system. They had chained themselves to a door handle in the Marlborough Street Court waiting room; the court was being temporarily held in Francis Street, Tottenham Court Road. Charged with obstruction, they gave obviously made-up names: Ann Smith, Edith Smith, Enuncita Smyth, Lilian Smyth, Louisa Smith; the one calling herself Ann Smith was in fact Nina Boyle. Evidence was given that the handle of the door to which they were chained was wrenched off by the police and the women removed from the building. When outside, they refused to go away. 'Ann Smith' said that in consequence of the rough manner in which the police ejected them one of her comrades was nearly killed. She almost fainted and it was impossible for the others to go away and leave her in that condition. Inspector Mansfield said that no more force was used than was necessary.

Upon the magistrate's ruling that a question in cross-examination was irrelevant, 'Ann Smith' remarked, 'Now, now, Mr Campbell, you must not do it. It's naughty.' A little later she said to the prosecutor, 'Would you mind not talking down your waistcoat, but speak up so that we can hear.' She later said to a police sergeant who was a witness in the case, 'I know it is not fashionable in this Court to tell the truth, but do try.' The women got the case adjourned by saying they wanted the Marlborough Street Court janitor called as a witness.

The arson campaign continued, with about half a dozen attacks each month. They occurred throughout the country; Scots involved included Arabella Scott who set fire to the stand at Kelso racecourse in April 1913, and was one of those who used the thirst strike as a means to obtain quick, if temporary, release, and Fanny Parker and Ethel Moorhead, who in July tried to blow up the cottage in Alloway where Robert Burns was born. Arson attacks in June and July 1914 included a mansion in High Wycombe, shops in Nottingham and London, Ballymenoch House in Ulster and Blaby railway station. In Durham, Constance Lewcock, a local schoolteacher, was responsible for burning down a railway building at Esh Winning; the actual act of arson was done by a miner supporter, Joss Craddock, while she had the perfect alibi of being at a public meeting! She was never charged, but was forced to leave her school. On 29 July, Newtownards race stand was attacked. In the seven months before the war, suffragettes were responsible for 107 incidents of arson, 111 of mutilation of works of art and 14 other 'outrages'.

The serious side of the struggle should never be forgotten; women were still using the weapon of the hunger strike, with all the horrors it involved. When Frances Gordon was released from Perth Prison after hunger striking, her condition was described as 'appalling. Like a famine victim – the skin brown, her face bones standing out, her eyes half shut – her voice a whisper, her hands quite cold, her pulse a thread – her wrist joints stiff and painful – this was not from rough handling but from poisoning. The breath was most offensive … and the contents of the bowel over which she had no control, were appalling.'

Everything changed on 4 August 1914; war was declared against Germany. Emmeline and Charlotte Pankhurst were strong supporters of the war and of the duty – and right – of women to fully participate in it. They declared an immediate truce and offered the services of their 'army' in this new cause. In return, all suffragette prisoners should be released at once. At first McKenna was cautious, offering only to release those prisoners who would undertake not to commit further outrages. However, on 10 August it was decided that all suffragette prisoners were to be unconditionally released. Though many suffragette groups followed the Pankhursts' lead, not every suffragette became a whole-hearted supporter of the war; a sizeable proportion considered the war to be wrong and took part in anti-war campaigns.

Many thousands of men volunteered to fight in the war, and in 1916 conscription was introduced; almost every male of military age was called up. Their places were taken by women who in this way gained jobs in engineering and other skilled work from which they had largely been excluded. Many worked in munitions, both dirty and dangerous work; several died during explosions in munitions factories. Other women supported the men in the front line, by driving trucks and performing similar work within the armed forces, and many women did vital work in a more traditional female occupation, nursing.

Many people think that women earned the right to vote because of the work they did in the war. As J. B. Priestley wrote, 'I am certain it was really the First World War itself that made further opposition to the women's vote clearly ridiculous. When girls and women had been making munitions and driving heavy lorries, it was no use telling them any longer that God and Nature intended them only to make ginger puddings and darn socks.' Even arch-opponent Prime Minister Asquith said on the death of Edith Cavell in

October 1915, 'She has taught the bravest man among us a lesson in supreme courage; yes, and in this United Kingdom and in the Dominions there are thousands of such women, but a year ago we did not know it.' As Mrs Fawcett said, 'pathetic blindness'; such courage had always been part of women's make-up, as the bravery of the suffragettes had shown. The door which the war pushed open had already been unlocked thanks to the activities of the suffragettes, whether militant or peaceful.

It had become unthinkable that women should not have the vote, and also that soldiers who were risking their lives for their country should be excluded from its franchise. In October 1916, an all-party conference met to consider franchise reform for the disenfranchised fighting men. In May 1917, the Representation of the People Bill, enfranchising all men and most women, was introduced to the Commons. The Bill easily passed through the House of Commons; when the House divided on the clause which enfranchised women, the vote was 385 to 55, that is 7 to 1 in favour and including a majority in favour in every political party. In the House of Lords, the vote was 134 in favour, 71 against. The royal assent was given on 6 February 1918; Millicent was present at the ceremony.

The law came into force in February 1918; women over the age of thirty who were householders or the wives of householders were enfranchised; about 6 million women out of 11 million now had the vote. The reason for this limitation was that, if all women were allowed the vote, then they would be in the majority as there are more women in the country than there are men; at the time this seemed a terrifying prospect to the all-male Parliament!

Women could now vote in parliamentary elections, but could they stand as candidates? The law was ambiguous and some women did put themselves forward at once. First in the field was Nina Boyle, who put herself forward for a by-election at Keighley. The returning officer declared her nomination papers out of order but stressed that this was not because she was a woman; had the papers been correct, he would have accepted them. In August, the first prospective candidate, Mary MacArthur, was adopted by the Labour Party at Stourbridge. On 23 October, Herbert Samuel proposed that a Bill be passed specifically making women eligible to become Members of Parliament. He proposed that any woman over twenty-one could stand, so that some women might become MPs even before they could vote! The vote in favour was 274 to 25 and the Bill received the royal assent in November.

This was only just in time; the general election was announced for 4 December. Seventeen female candidates were nominated – out of a total of 1,623 candidates for 707 seats. They included some of the suffragette leaders – Emmeline Pethick-Lawrence and Charlotte Despard for Labour, Violet Markham (who had been an active supporter of the anti-women's suffrage movement but was converted to the suffrage course during the war) as an Independent Liberal. Christabel Pankhurst, Edith How Martyn, Emily Phipps and Ray Strachey were among the women standing as Independents, Christabel being the only woman candidate to receive the 'coupon' as an approved supporter of the Lloyd George Government. However, none of these women were elected (Christabel coming closest at

Smethwick, where she polled over 8,000 votes, losing by just 775 votes) or indeed ever became Members of Parliament. The first woman actually to be elected to Parliament was the Countess Constance Markievicz, a Sinn Fein activist who fought her campaign from Holloway Prison, and made it clear that she had no intention of taking up her seat; she is supposed to have visited the House just once to look at her name engraved over a coat peg!

However, it was not long before the real first woman MP was elected; Nancy, Lady Astor, stood in Plymouth Sutton after her husband, the sitting MP, had been elevated to the Lords. The by-election took place on 15 November 1919 and Lady Astor received 14,495 votes, 5,000 more than her nearest opponent. She was introduced to the House on 1 December, entering the House with the Prime Minister (Lloyd George) and the leader of the Conservative party (A. J. Balfour) on either side of her. Ironically, she was American-born and had never taken any part in the struggle for the women's vote. Progress was slow but another twenty women were elected over the subsequent decade.

Many suffragettes were unhappy that women had not been given the vote on the same basis as men, but others saw that it was only a matter of time. In practice, it took a decade to achieve full equality. In 1928, the Representation of the People Act gave women the vote on the same terms as men. The so-called 'flapper vote' election saw sixty-nine female candidates, with seven new female MPs elected (very close to eight, Barbara Ayrton Gould losing at Northwich by just four votes!). The subsequent government, formed by James Ramsey MacDonald, included the first-ever woman Cabinet minister; Margaret Bondfield was appointed Minister of Labour. She had not been a suffragette, working instead for women's rights within the trade union movement. For the next seventy years most Cabinets had a female member – usually just one – but it was not until the late 1990s that a more reasonable number of women were regularly to be found at the Cabinet table.

Emmeline Pankhurst lived to see the fulfilment of her dream, dying on 14 June 1928. Millicent Fawcett died in the following year. Charlotte Despard was eighty-four in 1928, and her birthday party was an occasion for celebrating the victory. She pointed the way to the future, saying, 'I never believed that equal votes would come in my lifetime. But when an impossible dream comes true, we must go on to another.'

Some memorials to the suffragettes have appeared over the years. The statue of Emmeline Pankhurst in Victoria Tower Gardens in London was put up in 1930, just two years after her death. Speaking at its unveiling, the Prime Minister at the time, Stanley Baldwin, compared her to Martin Luther and Jean-Jacques Rousseau – people who were not the sum totals of the movements in which they took part, but who played crucial roles in the struggle for reform. Edith How Martyn formed the Suffragette Fellowship to perpetuate the memory of the movement. In 1970 they erected a memorial outside Caxton Hall (where many suffragette meetings had been held), near New Scotland Yard in London; designed by Edwin Russell, it was formally unveiled by Lilian Lenton.

However, the most important memorial lies in your hands if you are a woman. Give some thought to the sacrifices